Genetta,
R Family Dental
is the Best!!!

ROCHELLE MELANIE

LOOK WHAT Happened to My POCKET CHANGE!

Low- to Middle-Income Saving and Investing

LOOK WHAT HAPPENED TO MY POCKET CHANGE!
Low- to Middle- Income Saving and Investing

Copyright © 2014 Rochelle Melanie.

All rights reserved. No part of this book may be used or reproduced by any means, graphic, electronic, or mechanical, including photocopying, recording, taping or by any information storage retrieval system without the written permission of the publisher except in the case of brief quotations embodied in critical articles and reviews.

iUniverse books may be ordered through booksellers or by contacting:

iUniverse
1663 Liberty Drive
Bloomington, IN 47403
www.iuniverse.com
1-800-Authors (1-800-288-4677)

Because of the dynamic nature of the Internet, any web addresses or links contained in this book may have changed since publication and may no longer be valid. The views expressed in this work are solely those of the author and do not necessarily reflect the views of the publisher, and the publisher hereby disclaims any responsibility for them.

Any people depicted in stock imagery provided by Thinkstock are models, and such images are being used for illustrative purposes only.
Certain stock imagery © Thinkstock.

ISBN: 978-1-4917-3701-9 (sc)
ISBN: 978-1-4917-3703-3 (hc)
ISBN: 978-1-4917-3702-6 (e)

Library of Congress Control Number: 2014910861

Printed in the United States of America.

iUniverse rev. date: 07/28/14

In loving memory of my dearest friend in the world,
Darryl Ashanti Bydnum

(December 17, 1963–July 10, 2012)

CONTENTS

Acknowledgments ix
Introduction xi
Chapter 1   Where Does Wealth Come From? 1
Chapter 2   Why Life Needs Organization 7
Chapter 3   The Benefits of a Good Work Ethic 13
Chapter 4   Credit and Paying Your Bills 19
Chapter 5   Banks, Finance Companies, and Loan Stores ... 27
Chapter 6   Coupons, Rebates, Reward Points, and Dollar
            Stores 33
Chapter 7   The Real Savings Begin Here 39
Chapter 8   United States Savings Bonds 45
Chapter 9   Mutual Funds 51
Chapter 10 The Stock Market 55
Chapter 11 Real Estate 67
Chapter 12 401(k), Deferring Income 71
Chapter 13 Investing with Life Insurance 77
The End Result 83

ACKNOWLEDGMENTS

I WOULD LIKE TO GIVE MANY thanks to my family and friends, who have been supportive to me in this very special endeavor. I would like to first thank my parents, Mildred and Eddie, who have always given me the loving support necessary to encourage me to reach for the sky. I want to give thanks to the world's greatest siblings—Millicent, Earnestine, and Eddie Jr.—each of whom I dearly love. Jeremy, Melanie, Lasalle, and Mylin—I love you guys! Mr. Curtis, thanks for being a part of our wonderful family. Special thanks to Ms. Karen Rodgers for all of your love and patience during the writing of this book. Ms. Stacy Muse, thank you for always reminding me that I have a wealth of financial knowledge that needs to be shared with the world. Mr. Ned Dinkins, thanks for always asking me when you are going to be able to read my book. And lastly, Ms. Jen Valle, you are my very first reader. I'm very happy that reading my work was a great financial learning experience for you. Your comments are very inspiring and appreciated. Thanks for all of your loving support.

INTRODUCTION

WHY WOULD YOU WANT TO read a personal savings and investing book by Rochelle Melanie when there are countless other options available with respect to saving and investing?

As a minority American female, I believe that my approach to savings and investments is something that anyone can adopt. I did not do any research to write *Look What Happened to My Pocket Change!*; I simply described my spending, saving, and investing techniques for creating personal financial stability.

I eventually made it to the million-dollar level with my assets. I live well, but in comparison to the average rich American, I do not consider myself to be wealthy because a million dollars in assets can accumulate without liquidity. The lifestyle of a wealthy American is usually lavish and often without financial concern. Living as an average middle-class individual is good enough for me. I will always work toward my goals—no matter what level I have reached. Was this hard for me to accomplish since I started off with very little financial resources and knowledge? No! Anyone can accomplish this. No matter what you earn, you can save. If you learn to live below your means, you will have already accomplished half the battle in terms of becoming financially stable.

During America's national debt crisis and worldwide recession, I purchased a new BMW. I remodeled my home.

I remodeled my rental properties, and I took my usual five annual vacations. All my bills are paid by the beginning of the month—before they are due. I deposit money into my savings and investment accounts. I have increased my contribution to my company's 401(k) plan from 10 percent to 15 percent. Most importantly, I did all the things I would have done if the national debt crisis had not happened.

The national debt crisis and worldwide recession were only a couple of reasons why I decided to write *Look What Happened to My Pocket Change!*. These unfortunate events did not have to affect a person in any way. They did not need to have any bearing on the life a person can become accustomed to living. As the world struggles through its financial crises, many Americans are affected by high unemployment rates. People are losing their homes, financial debt is escalating, and major companies are filing for bankruptcy. Many small businesses are closing, and people's lives are being affected in negative ways. But why should this be your struggle if it does not have to be?

I know that *Look What Happened to My Pocket Change!* can help millions of low- to middle-income individuals change their attitudes about spending, saving, and investing. *Look What Happened to My Pocket Change!* is geared toward low- to middle-income people who are struggling with their finances, and it does not matter how much they earn. I do not consider myself wealthy in comparison to others, but my lifestyle is very prosperous because I do not live from pay check to pay check. I do not have financial burdens and I can afford many of the finer things that life has to offer. In the beginning of my career, I earned minimum wage. I now earn a decent salary, but I took advantage of saving and investing whenever I could. I cut corners, lived below my means, and utilized the bare necessities. I did not try to live above my means. I made a plan, stayed on course, saved, and achieved my goals.

Look What Happened to My Pocket Change! is based upon my experiences. To begin my savings and investing program, I saved all my pocket change and placed it in a piggy bank every day. When my piggy bank became too small, I purchased a larger container with a sealed cap. At the end of my first year of saving pocket change, I took my coins to the bank and opened a passbook savings account. A passbook savings account is an account that requires a person to bring in a bankbook every time a deposit or withdrawal is made. The deposit or withdrawal is recorded into the book as a receipt of the transaction.

After I established my passbook saving account, I deposited ten dollars every week from my paycheck—before any bills were paid. As my salary increased, I increased my weekly deposits. When I received bonuses, I deposited these additional funds into my passbook savings account whenever possible. I accomplished this by not making plans for funds that came via raises or bonuses. I continued to live as I always had. The secret to saving more was that my living expenses did not increase just because my salary increased. If I had lived on a certain amount of money before, there was no reason why I could not continue to live on that same amount and save the rest of what I earned.

My next step was investing in United States savings bonds,

which I purchased every month after all my bills were paid. I increased the value every year, but I still saved my pocket change and made deposits into my passbook savings account. After the maturity dates on my savings bonds increased, I decided to be more aggressive. I cashed in all my accumulated savings bonds and purchased mutual funds. My mutual funds did well, and I did not have to watch them closely because fund managers monitored the performance.

I decided to be even more aggressive. I started trading in the stock market, which became exceptionally lucrative, and my annual income doubled. However, after the stock market became unstable, I had to adopt a more stable strategy. I started to purchase investment properties. Even though the rental income was good, I did not stop there. I started investing in life insurance.

Most low- to middle-income individuals think that the only way to manage finances and live comfortably is to be wealthy and financially savvy—or at least understand all the subtle nuances of saving and investing. They also believe that their annual incomes must be at a certain level in order to start saving or investing. Even though these concerns are valid, they are not the most important factors in becoming financially stable or free of debts.

The leading misconception for most low- to middle-income individuals is that a person must have assets that range in the millions of dollars in order to live comfortably. *Look What Happened to My Pocket Change!* is not about becoming a millionaire or wealthy; it is about living well without being wealthy. If a person is financially stable, it is possible to live well. Most low- to middle-income individuals do not understand the simple techniques of finance.

To become financially secure, people do not need financial backgrounds. They don't need to be financially savvy or earn a lot of money. They simply have to know what to do with the money they earn. *Look What Happened to My Pocket Change!* is about making prudent financial decisions. This book is about putting things in perspective.

An important factor in saving is trying to live below one's means, but this does not require living in poverty or going to bed hungry. It does not mean that people should go without basic necessities; it means that they should try to survive with the basic necessities until financial goals are met. Being financially successful is simple, but it requires awareness that this has to be achieved in steps.

While enjoying a weekend off from work, I was conversing with several of my friends. They asked why I had been so busy and how I was able to pay for my increased expenses while the rest of America was in a recession. These questions hit me like a ton of bricks. I had not realized that the economy had affected so many of my relatives, friends, and acquaintances. Many of them were losing their jobs and homes. I knew that the world's debt crisis was a concern, but I was in a financially stable situation. These crises were other people's problems. I had positioned myself so well that the crisis had not affected me in any way. After several similar conversations, I concluded that I had a compelling story that was worth sharing.

Several of my friends earn more than one hundred thousand dollars a year, but they have asked to borrow money from me. I could not understand this. It took some time to realize that I earned less, but I had a much higher net worth than they did. I decided to do a survey. I asked my well-to-do friends what they would do if they had an emergency and needed $10,000 or $20,000 in cash within a couple of weeks. None of them would be able to raise the money. My findings took me by total surprise. I was amazed. I could not comprehend being single and childless and not being able to come up with this amount of money in a couple of weeks to address an emergency. I was making half the salary of my friends, but I would still be able to come up with that money in an emergency. After completing my survey, I was convinced that I could offer something of value to many people by sharing my financial knowledge.

My personal experiences led to financial stability. *Look What Happened to My Pocket Change!* does not cater to the rich; it is intended to help low- to middle-class working people—just like you and me—to live well without being wealthy. There are many resources available with respect to personal finances, but I'm giving it to you straight! It does not make a difference how much you earn or what you do for a living. When it comes to saving and investing, a goal is a goal. The best way to achieve your goal is to attack it from every possible direction. People will have to adjust their lifestyles, but the financial stability will be worth it.

Finance does not have to be complicated, tedious, or taxing. The fact that I did not realize that the United States was in a recession was reason enough for me to write *Look What Happened to My Pocket Change!* The financial projects I undertook during these times confirmed my beliefs, and the questions I posed to my friends convinced me to write *Look What Happened to My Pocket Change!* I did not write this book to cash in on the profits. My story can help lots of low- to middle-income individuals understand saving, investing, and living well. This information is valuable to anyone who reads *Look What Happened to My Pocket Change!*.

I want to pass on some simple tips that will make people more financially stable. A person does not have to be a rocket scientist or a Wall Street professional. This person just has to be willing to make some sacrifices, adjustments, and wiser decisions when it comes to spending, saving, and investing.

I often peruse bookstores for the next best financial read, and it is rare to come across a financial book written by a minority. It is even rarer to find one written by a female minority. I can relate to how low- to middle-income individuals think about finances; a common point of reference can be helpful. Low- to middle-income individuals with limited resources and limited financial knowledge will relate to my method of saving and investing with no difficulties. Most investment books are designed for wealthy, innovative, savvy, and experienced investors, but *Look What Happened to My Pocket Change!* caters to the average American who struggles with living from paycheck to paycheck.

A lot of finance books tell people how to save and invest, but they do not provide, in detail, the appropriate resources in terms of how to actually get started or how little a person will need to get started, which are important topics. *Look What Happened to My Pocket Change!* provides all of this easily and efficiently while allowing for a desirable lifestyle. By following my easy step-by-step techniques—while incorporating one's own financial knowledge—a person will quickly learn that there is no big secret to becoming financially stable. Individuals will also learn to save and invest without noticing the deductions from their incomes. By gradually increasing the amounts they save, people will achieve their goals without diminishing the quality of life for their families. Anyone can be taught to save and invest without being deprived of the bare necessities.

My lifestyle is nothing short of middle class. I created my financial net worth through the techniques I discuss in *Look What Happened to My Pocket Change!*. I'm not an inventor. I'm not a business owner. I have never inherited a large sum of money or won the lottery. I'm an average American who works every day to earn a living. I started my career earning a minimum wage. I attribute my current financial stability to being dedicated to saving, investing, and controlling my spending. I always say, "It's not about how much you earn; it's what you do with what you earn." With a salary of less than $10,000, a person still has the chance to save and invest. If a person makes saving and investing a priority, it is possible to enjoy the benefits of all the finer things that life has to offer.

I will always continue to work toward my goals. I want to ensure that life is as comfortable as possible for myself and my family. Living life and enduring all of life's obstacles is a complicated process. With the right resources, most people can determine their own financial futures. I'm providing financial knowledge in a way that everyone can comprehend.

A person may think that saving coins will equate to nothing in this day and age, but it's a start. I do not minimize any amount when it comes to savings. *Look What Happened to My Pocket Change!* is about low- to middle-income investing. A lot of people earn twice my salary, but they have massive debts. Other people are in two-income households, struggling to pay their bills every month. I can teach people like this how to spend, save, and invest on any salary; eventually, they will not have to live paycheck to paycheck.

'M JUST LIKE YOU! I was born and raised on the West Side of Chicago. I grew up with my parents, Mildred and Eddie, in the same household and three siblings, Millie, Eddie, and Ernie. I love my family dearly.

People never forget certain things from growing up. For me, those things always had something to do with my parents. My parents tried to be strict, but when parents are away, the children will play. Just like other children in the 1970s, as soon our parents were not around, my siblings and I would do all the things we were told not to do. The things we did as children were never illegal, only mischievous. We made sure that we were in bed and sound asleep before our parents made it back home from a night out on the town.

The thing I remember most is that my parents were always very compassionate when it came to their children. My parents gave us what we needed, although not necessarily what we wanted. Their job was to provide shelter, food, clothing, education, love, and discipline until we were adults, but the rest would be up to us. As a child, I could not comprehend the difference between providing us with what we needed and what we wanted. I thought what we wanted was the same as what we needed. As an adult, however, I fully appreciate the distinction. When I look back on those years, I know that if we had been given everything we wanted, we would not have been able to achieve what we really wanted in life.

There were times when we did get a little of what we asked for: I cannot remember my parents—especially my father—ever saying no to me whenever I asked for a dollar. On one very hot summer day, I spent all day riding my bike with the other children in the neighborhood. We decided to go to the candy store to get potato chips and snow cones. I raced to the house to find my dad. He had a full-time job with General Motors and owned a body and fender repair shop that he operated during the evening and on weekends. I went inside, but he was gone. My mother was out shopping.

I did not have any money, but I decided to tag along with the other children anyway. Tagging along with the other children taught me the most valuable lesson of my young life. I quickly learned that children may be fun to play with, but they also can be very cruel. I stood with all the other children while they were eating potato chips, candy, and snow cones, and none of them would share any treats with me. I was the only child without snacks because my mom and dad had not been at home. For some reason, that experience changed me. I remember the experience as if it were yesterday.

At the age of ten, I decided to never again be in an insolvent situation. Out of all my wonderful childhood memories, this one recollection haunted me for a long time. I know that it was just bad timing that my parents were not around when I wanted to ask them for money, but I still experienced such an empty feeling in my stomach. That feeling left a deep imprint on my memory.

Three years later, I got a job at the local toy store. In the past thirty years, I have never been unemployed or broke again. If someone is determined to be financially stable, almost nothing can stop a person from fulfilling that goal. I had a very strong influence while growing up with both parents in the same household. My mother was very passionate about life, and my dad lived life to the fullest. My parents went to work every day, and they were both proud to be employed by good companies. General Motors and the food manufacturer my mother worked for both paid very decent wages for that time. I cannot recall a time when my mother or father complained about going to work to provide for our family. They both knew what had to be done to support a family of six. I honestly believe that I have the best parents anyone could possibly have. They laid a very strong foundation that has allowed me to prosper in many ways.

Today, I'm all grown up and enjoying life to the fullest. I have been employed with the same financial institution for more than twenty-five years. I love fancy sports cars. I have owned several beautiful sports cars in my lifetime. My current car is a beautiful BMW hardtop convertible. I have several properties in the beautiful western suburbs of Illinois. I take as many as five vacations per year, including international travels. I enjoy the latest fashions and dine at some of the finest restaurants. Most importantly, my life is financially secure.

My career has enhanced my lifestyle in a variety of ways, but I attribute most of my financial success to my style of spending, saving, and investing. My smart style of saving allows me do whatever I want, however I want, and often whenever I want. I have never lived from paycheck to paycheck or been dependent on an income tax refund.

I feel that everyone is entitled to live the lifestyle that he or she desires, but there are sacrifices that have to be made if a person wants to live comfortably. I discuss the things that I have accomplished only in a manner of knowing that the compromises I made were not as complex as the outcome would lead you to believe. People may think that what I achieved was easier said than done, but it was not hard to accomplish.

I HAVE SPENT THE PAST TWENTY-FIVE years in the financial industry. I started out as a teller. I was straight out of high school and eager to learn everything about finances. I attended college while working full-time to make certain that I was prepared for any opportunities that came my way. During the past twenty-five years, I have advanced in my career. I have had continuous financial education and training as it related to consumer banking products, lending, investing, trusts, and financial planning. I have earned financial certificates, investment licenses, and a life insurance license. I have been a top producer and assisted in managing a banking center for one of the largest financial institutions in the United States. My financial experience and knowledge have allowed me to view finances with a very comprehensible perspective. There are so many intricacies that surround finances, and I have mastered a lot of the particulars while still learning every day.

My financial background is not the primary reason why I have succeeded. If I had not gone into in the financial field, I still would have made the same choices about spending, saving, and investing. There is one thing that I would like to make clear from the beginning. I did not write this book because I work for one of the largest financial institutions in the United States, and that is not the primary reason why I am able to live well. While cleaning out my files, I came across my first income tax return. My gross income was $7,600, but I still lived well back then.

In my many years of working and saving, I have learned a very valuable and important lesson about wealth. How much a person earns is not what matters; what is important is what the individual does with his or her earnings. I cannot stress this proven fact enough. My work background prepared me for the world of finance. I gained knowledge about saving, investing, trading stocks, purchasing bonds, selecting mutual funds and options, and managing a 401(k).

The ability to live well is the focus of *Look What Happened to My Pocket Change!*. With the right knowledge and education, it is easy to live well. This is what I'm sharing. The average person was not born with a silver spoon in his or her mouth, and neither was I. I made a solid plan, stuck to it, and prospered—and so can you. I mentioned my accomplishments because they were not hard to attain, and I have always dreamed of sharing the little things that the wealthy will not share.

I love the world of finance, and I want the world to know that it is not as hard as the financial gurus make it out to be. I think that all people would like to make their lives as easy as possible, and this can be achieved with a solid plan of action. The average American believes that the good life is only for the rich and famous, but this is not true. Reading this book, understanding that I'm just like you, and following this well-constructed path can lead a person to good living.

I have wanted to write this book for several years, but as everyone knows, life can speed by in the blink of an eye. I thought that most low- to middle-income individuals also possessed the knowledge I had acquired. After realizing that this was not always true, I was compelled to share my story to help as many low- to middle-income individuals as possible become more financially stable. This book is for low- to middle-income individuals who struggle with managing money and find it difficult to save. Low- to middle-income individuals will learn how to create wealth, overcome obstacles that prevent them from saving and investing, and manage money better. These techniques for wise investing, smart borrowing, and getting organized will enhance their lifestyles.

The media and financial institutions make finance look extremely complicated, but the behind-the-scenes work is not all that difficult. When people feel that something is going to be complex or challenging, they typically avoid it and look for easier ways out. Once low- to middle-income individuals comprehend the dynamics of saving and investing, they can become more at ease and less apprehensive. Managing personal finances while saving and investing can be as simple as writing a check to pay a bill.

Many Americans need to take the time to understand the obstacles that seem to make finances difficult. If they do not understand the significant role that money plays in our lives, things can be tremendously tough.

People say, "Money is not everything," "Money is the root to all evil," and "Nothing good can come from having a lot of money."

I disagree to some extent with these phrases. I say, "Money

only matters when you do not have it," "Evil surrounds money, but we have the power to control it," and "Having money can create a lot of good if it's utilized in the correct way."

I know these aphorisms are simply opinions and depend on how each person thinks, but the bottom line is that people cannot live without money. Why not make this existence comfortable since life is short and no one can predict when it will end?

CHAPTER 1
Where Does Wealth Come From?

MOST PEOPLE THINK THAT GOING to work every day and working hard are the main elements that make up wealth. Some people even think that holding down two jobs will secure their financial futures. Most people do not know that working from nine to five and grueling hours of overtime are the least effective ways for the average American to gain the financial wealth that can contribute to a secure future.

Hard work alone will not allow the average low- to middle-income individual to live well or control debt. For the past twelve years, I have worked in the private sector for high-net worth individuals. In the private sector, individuals can have assets ranging up to a billion dollars. It has been my experience that many affluent Americans gained their wealth from inheritance, insurance payouts, or lawsuits. The Americans who have acquired wealth from hard work are usually inventors. These inventors who have created their wealth from hard work have mastered a certain product that is beneficial to people's everyday existence.

Do not misunderstand me when I say that working hard at a job is not the way to financial success, but it is one of the least effective ways to achieve financial success without savings and investing. Clearly, there are doctors, lawyers, Wall Street professionals, accountants, entrepreneurs, and private contractors, among many others, who have been successful at securing financial wealth. On average, however, these white-collar professionals hold PhDs, master's degrees, or CFA and CPA licenses, etc.

This book focuses on the low- to middle-income individual, the blue-collar workers, the minimum wagers, the low- to middle-income earners, the working middle class, the poor, and the less fortunate. Being dedicated to an employer while working hard every day will usually help a person support a family and perhaps allow for an annual vacation, but without the proper savings and investing tools, it's is very hard to become financially stable.

Most lower- to middle-income Americans do not know that the wealthy will always have an advantage because they are surrounded by financial resources that enrich their lives. These financial resources have afforded them the finest educations, the best jobs, the best networking connections, and the greatest life experiences. Since average lower- to middle-income Americans cannot compete with that, they have to be realistic and approach their financial goals in practical ways. They have to set smaller goals to achieve their bigger goals. This book describes the many different phases of spending, saving, and investing in a manner that will fit into any budget. I have found ways to save and become comfortable with my financial stability.

Minorities do not typically have the luxury of inheriting trust funds from their parents, grandparents, aunts, or uncles or benefiting from life insurance or large sums of money from a lawsuit. Since they will always be at a disadvantage, they will have to work harder and smarter. There are many ways to approach building wealth, and the first approach is stabilizing finances. In order to do this, a person's mental and physical states should be in order. What does mental and physical well-being have to do with achieving financial wealth? Most simply stated, having positive energy sends signals to a person's brain to help creative thinking. Being physically fit provides energy that can be exerted in daily activities. This combination makes it easier to plan future goals strategically. Realistically, how can people take care of financial affairs if their physical and mental states are not at their best? Mental and physical states play an important role in achieving well-being and obtaining stability in life. With stability, it is possible to keep goals in line and not steer off the determined path. These stabilities will create a solid foundation, which can strengthen concentration and dedication for something an individual really wants to achieve. Essentially, if a person is determined and focuses, it is highly predictable that he or she will attain their financial goal in life.

I elaborated about the creation of wealth, and I mentioned that wealth is often inherited. Very few low- to middle-income individuals pass down significant financial wealth because they do not have the knowledge about creating financial wealth; therefore, we struggle with building our finances. It's important to create wealth because it can be passed down to the next generation. Building wealth to pass on to the next generation can be as simple as educating youths about spending, saving and investing. This type of education can help cultivate logical thinking as it relates to establishing financial goals. Also, being proactive, as opposed to being inactive will prepare the next generation for even greater success.

Building wealth to pass on to the next generation can consist of educating through the development of strategies about spending, saving and investing, thereby helping to cultivate logical thinking concerning life goals and being proactive, as opposed to being inactive and neglecting to prepare the next generation for success.

Dedication and striving for more helps a person build a solid financial foundation. Having a concrete financial plan allows people to achieve their goals. Starting out small should never be a concern. I am a firm believer that when starting out small, the value of money can become more appreciated;

therefore, people will eventually make better financial decisions in their lives. Low- to middle-income individuals must learn that educating the next generation financially will encourage success beyond measure.

Low- to middle-income individuals also need to understand how to maintain wealth that is inherited. Many of us have known someone who inherited a small fortune from parents, grandparents, aunts, or uncles, but they lost it all in a very short period of time. They ended up broke because they did not know how to manage their finances or lacked the proper education about how to spend, save, or invest to maintain the value of an inheritance.

It is never too soon to begin teaching the next generation. I have two nieces (Melanie and Lasalle), a nephew (Jeremy), and a great-nephew (Mylin). At six years old, Mylin is very smart. Like most children his age, he often says some of the most unexpected and funniest things. Mylin is a strangely intelligent boy. He likes to repeat things that he hears, both good and bad. This is the time in a child's life when vital learning takes place.

Whenever I spend time with Mylin, I talk to him about finances. Perhaps it seems extreme to talk about finances with a six year old, but this is a very impressionable time in his life. While Mylin may not understand what I'm trying to convey to him, he surely hears me; eventually he will start to digest what I'm conveying. As he gets older, his curiosity will have already been piqued. I'm waiting for the day when he comes to me and asks about spending, savings, and investing in stocks, bonds, and mutual funds. When thinking that someone is too young to learn, it is time to think again. This is how to build a solid foundation. When someone thinks there is nothing to pass on, it is time to think again.

People often reflect about things they have done wrong financially and wonder what they could have done to prevent them. Knowing what one has done wrong and coming up with a way to correct the problem is half the battle. In life, there will be financial mistakes, obstacles, and headaches. People cannot avoid these things. The important thing to remember about finances it that it is a continuous process. Passing down financial knowledge will help prevent the next generation from repeating common financial mistakes.

Knowledge about how to obtain financial wealth can teach the next generation to achieve financial goals. If low- to middle-income individuals do not have the riches to pass down to the next generation, they can have the resources to jump-start the next generation. I cannot stress enough how important it is for low- to middle-income individuals to start building financial wealth. Low- to middle-income individuals can create great wealth by adopting certain economic practices.

CHAPTER 2
Why Life Needs Organization

ORGANIZATION PLAYS A SIGNIFICANT ROLE in building financial wealth. A person whose personal life isn't in order will probably not have his or her finances in order without the help of a financial advisor, which can be very costly. To achieve financial goals, one's physical state will play a vital role. Waking up every morning and feeling good will elevate a person's self-esteem and confidence. This will promote the ability to achieve financial goals in life.

A person who wakes up rested, energized, and ready to tackle the world will be stronger, which will lead to the possibility of having a productive day. Someone who wakes up grumpy and dreads getting out of bed has a good chance of carrying that attitude throughout the day, which will surely lower productivity. A person's mood is a very important part of productivity. That is why it's important to start the day fully rested with a positive attitude—even if you are going to work as a french fry chef at a fast-food restaurant. It is important to remember that a person's current position in life is only a stepping-stone to a better life. A person must fuel success; what is better than waking up every morning refreshed, energized, and ready to be productive?

Positive influences and the company one keeps should be reflections of how that person wants to live. This is the most significant statement I have ever heard. When someone is trying to accomplish goals in life, that person needs all the positive energy that can be gathered. A constant flow of positive energy will keep creative juices flowing. Negative energy is a goal buster because misery loves company. If a person is miserable, it is difficult to get in the mood to be creative; the last thing that person wants is to think about financial potential.

Think about positivity as growth and negativity as broke! This is all the more reason for people to seek out positive influences. People like to think that they are always in charge of their attitudes, moods, and feelings, but almost everyone has woken up in a wonderful mood and had their positive mood disrupted by someone else's negativity. As much as we would like to think that we are in control of our own feelings, to a certain degree, we are not. Since negativity can crush dreams and goals, it is important to surround yourself with as many positive people as possible.

Another part of being organized is working out. It is great to wake up rested, energized, and ready to tackle the day, but one does not want to fizzle out during the day. A physical workout can strengthen a person's productivity. Maintaining a high energy level throughout the day is essential for success. Working out keeps the body healthy and makes the blood flow freely. It keeps the arteries free from blockage, which can reduce stress and decrease the chances of developing heart disease.

Working out gives the body the energy it needs to tackle day-to-day obstacles. Energy motivates the brain; it allows a person to think outside the normal range of daily activity. Working out broadens expectations and expands creativity. I cannot stress enough the importance of keeping the body healthy. Americans should strive for at least thirty minutes of physical activity each day in order to maintain an optimum level of energy.

The average American may not know this, but physical activity is possible anywhere and at any time. When I get off the train in the morning, I take the stairs instead of the elevator. I find it amazing that I'm the only person taking the stairs. When I look around and see the sizes of many people riding the escalators, I'm often stunned. I find it even more amazing when people ask me why I take the stairs when they clearly should be taking the stairs with me. I do understand that everyone's health circumstances are different, but if a person makes a concerted effort toward a little physical activity every day, that person would be amazed at what he or she can accomplish.

When I'm at work, I often stretch in my chair or do chair exercises while working on the computer. I do leg extensions, crunches, and triceps and bicep twists. I often get up to walk around, and I take advantage of long walks on my lunch breaks. It is amazing how many physical activities a person can engage in during eight hours at work.

I cannot stress enough the significance of getting proper rest. I need it more because I have always been active. I have never really taken the time to sit back and relax because I always felt that I would miss out on a big opportunity. I have always made time for vacations, but I seldom made time for relaxing at home, doing nothing, or taking naps.

I have often made fun of people for napping every day, especially my sister Earnie. I have always had the notion that naps were strictly for babies and senior citizens because they do not have the energy to be vigorous all day long. I have never had the proper rest, and although I cannot go back and change the past, I can work on correcting the future. If I had a chance to go back and reconstruct my sleeping habits, I would definitely find a way to incorporate rest and relaxation into my life. I want to do this because my friends who have always incorporated the proper rest and relaxation—including daily naps—look like they have been drinking from the fountain of youth.

Karen has been my close friend for seven years. She has always made it a top priority to get at least ten hours of sleep each night. On her days off, she sleeps even more. When I first met her and learned of her sleeping habits, I thought something was terribly wrong with her because she would sometimes sleep more than she was awake during a day. I learned that she had incorporated her rest into her life many years earlier. I viewed this as being a negative, and I often teased her about the amount of sleep her body required because it appeared unproductive to me. However, Karen is very productive according to her lifestyle. Most importantly, because of her sleep habits, she is healthy. It looks as if time has stood still for her. She looks as if she is in her early thirties. She is in her mid forties. She is youthful, beautiful and doesn't have a gray hair on her head. I have several other friends who are in this same category who have gotten the proper amount of rest in their lives, and they look as if time has stood still for them too.

Eating right is another major part of being organized. Helping one's body function at its highest peak will allow a person to perform at the highest possible level. Breakfast is the most essential meal of the day because it fuels the start of the day. I have often noticed that when I start my day with a high-protein breakfast, things seem to go smoother. People should aim for three balanced meals per day, but this can vary depending on the individual. I have noticed that waiting until I am at the point of being very hungry before I eat my first meal can have an adverse effect because I will consume almost anything and any amount. Waiting until this point is not advisable because eating the first thing that is available is usually the wrong choice, and then wrong choices are typically made for the duration of the day. Watching what one eats is just as vital as eating three balanced meals. I also try not to eat if I'm not hungry, but I will have a snack to prevent me from making the wrong choices.

The environment plays a role in being organized. If a person wakes up every morning in a well organized environment, meaning if their home is free from clutter and distractions, this could help to prepare a person for a positive and productive work day. Home is the one place where people go to relax and unwind. If someone can manage to have structure in the place where the most time is spent, everything else will fall into place. It is hard to have one's home free of clutter, especially if there are children, but a person who keeps some type of organization in the home will relax better, prepare better, and be more productive in the outside world.

When it is time to relax and unwind, a person's environment can contribute to a sense of order. Children can be taught organization at a very early age, which can assist in the structuring of a home environment. Everyone in a household can play a role in keeping the home environment organized and free of stress. Rules have to be set and enforced at all times; the rules can be set with rewards in place that can encourage 100 percent participation. The same organization can be applied to vehicles.

The cleanliness of a vehicle can say a lot about the owner. Americans spend a lot of time in their vehicles, and their vehicles are often a reflection of them. I'm not saying that a person's home and vehicle have to be immaculate because this is hard to achieve for most people, but they should be orderly to reflect the level of financial success that a person is trying to achieve. These organizational factors are important for building a positive financial future. These organizational factors will not be achieved in the same way for everyone, but attempts should be made to create organization in life.

CHAPTER 3
The Benefits of a Good Work Ethic

WORKING IS ESSENTIAL TO BUILDING financial wealth because people need income in order to start saving loose change. Good work habits include always being on time or early for work, which allows a person time to prepare for the workday. Having a little extra time before the workday starts allows a person to be refreshed; it also allows time to properly adjust and plan ahead. Taking a few minutes before starting the day can be a productive way to prioritize a schedule, and it allows a person to manage the workload and achieve daily goals.

Furthermore, dressing for success is important. A person who looks good also feels good, and the quality produced is usually good. A person who feels professional will produce professionally. It should not make a difference what someone does for a living; it is a person's job to create a personal style. Dressing for success is not just a statement; it is a fact. A person who comes to work on time and is dressed appropriately gets noticed and stands out. When I was a teller, I knew that the position was a stepping-stone for me. I knew I would not be a teller for long. It was just the position I needed to get my foot in the door. Since I was thirteen, I wanted to have a career in banking. I arrived at work early every day.

I noticed that the manager always dressed very professionally and conducted herself in a professional manner. I watched her interactions with customers, and I had conversations with her about career paths within the organization. When my manager noticed that I had a sincere interest in the bank and my job, she decided to take me under her wing despite the fact that I had only been on the job for ninety days. There were many other employees who had been there much longer than I had.

She said, "No matter what position you are in, always come to work looking your best: dress for success." The day after that conversation, I came to work dressed as professionally as possible, and I continued to do so throughout my career. When I came to work as a teller, I dressed as a manager. I was always on time. I smiled all day long. I perfected my job. I volunteered for projects, and I was open to learning anything and everything that came my way.

After less than a year on the teller line, my manager promoted me to customer service representative. As a customer service representative, I had more personal contact with the customers and increased work responsibilities. I came to work early, dressed for success, and performed my job to the best of my ability.

In less than a year, my manager promoted me to personal banker. In two years, I progressed from being a teller to a being a personal banker. I was amazed by what I had accomplished in a very short time. I followed my manager's advice about dressing for success, always had an open mind, and was willing to learn from someone who was in the position I wanted to eventually occupy.

I spent a few years developing as a personal banker, and my manager was very supportive and happy about my performance. After several years in the personal banker role, I was ready for a new adventure. There was no managerial position available at my current location, but I decided to search positions at other locations within the bank. My manager did not want me to leave her location, but she knew that I was ready for the next step in my career. She advised me until I landed a senior banker/assisting manager position at one of the company's largest banking facilities on the North Side of Chicago. I brought all the knowledge and experience I had acquired in my previous positions and was very successful.

I took full advantage of every opportunity that was presented to me. I took on new challenges every day. The bank implemented some changes, and many of us had to obtain a life insurance license and a Series 6 & 63 license to sell mutual funds. Both licenses were difficult to obtain. No one in my banking center was willing to devote the time and effort to study for the exams. Since no employee was willing to step forward—and I was the senior person in charge and the only minority at my location—I decided to step forward and give it a try.

Studying for the exams and maintaining full-time duties at work was very demanding and challenging. After cramming a year of studying into four months, I passed all my exams and became a first line officer, assistant bank manager, and a senior top-producing banker at a branch of the largest bank in the United States. I was the only minority at my location, which was not an easy task, and I had the least amount of seniority. My colleagues struggled with my success until I eventually won them over.

After several successful years at that position, it was time for my next adventure. I learned to never become stagnant in my career. I did not want to become obsolete. I learned to always keep moving. My next move was to the Private Banking Department. Private banking is where most employees would like to end up in their banking careers. Private banking is where the high-net worth client is serviced. Individual client accounts ranged from a million dollars up to a billion dollars. I have been in the private banking sector for the past twelve years, and I'm still learning every day. When I initially joined the private banking sector of my company, it was my goal to become a client of the Private Banking Department. It has not happened yet, but I'm still working toward that goal.

In the Private Banking Department, I learned that hard work does not create wealth by itself. I learned that the majority of these clients' wealth came from inheritances, insurance proceeds, lawsuits, inventions, and hard work combined with proper spending, savings, and investing. On a daily basis, I interact with clients who have assets that can range as high as one billion dollars. The majority of them have inherited money, and their benefactors started off with small investments. If the money came from insurance polices, the policies were created over a long period at affordable rates. If the money came from lawsuits, it was put into a trust until the beneficiary attained the proper age—or the clients saved every dime possible and made the proper investments.

Going above and beyond one's job duties is a must for maintaining a position within a company—and that is how people get promoted. When someone comes to work with the right attitude, the chances of success are enhanced. Many Americans do not have their dream jobs, but people must do what they can to pay the bills. A person can look at a job as being undesirable and simply come to work every day feeling miserable and doing only what is expected—or a person can come to work prepared to do the job that he or she has been paid to do as well as possible while making plans to obtain a dream job or career.

People should always appreciate what they have and make the best of it until they can afford to make the necessary changes. I often say that hard work is not what makes a person wealthy, but the income it generates can be the basis that is needed to start saving and investing. This method and time can build financial stability, which will allow a person to live well without being wealthy. As I mentioned previously, most wealth comes from inheritance, insurance proceeds, lawsuits and inventions that have been handed down from generation to generation. In most cases where wealth was created from working a nine to five job that person utilized proper savings and investing techniques.

CHAPTER 4
Credit and Paying Your Bills

CREDIT IS IMPORTANT WHEN YOU are trying to create financial stability because even the wealthy have to apply for credit from time to time. Having cash available is always the preferred method, but there are many items that the average American will not have the cash to purchase. Therefore, maintaining a perfect credit history is imperative. I maintain several credit cards, but I do not carry any balances on them. I use them for emergencies. If I lose my job and am no longer able to pay my bills, I can live off my credit cards until I find another job. I would, however, utilize my savings first to pay my bills and provide me with everyday living funds. I would only tap into my available credit if necessary.

I do not recommend doing this; the rotation method is something that has to be planned out precisely and should only be used to address an emergency situation. I would pay the minimum balance due on all my bills with credit card A. I would use credit card B to pay the minimum balance due on credit card A. I would use credit card A to pay the minimum balance due on credit card B, which would have a much smaller balance because credit card B only covered the minimum balance due on credit card A.

Depending on the amount of available credit—while maintaining a good credit score—a person can utilize only two credit cards. As the years pass, you can introduce a third credit card to the rotation. In order to properly rotate credit card payments, a person would have to be very strategic about the timing of when to pay the amount due on a credit card using a different credit card. I watched a family member live for five years while unemployed by rotating payments between credit cards. Ideally, things may never come to this, but no one can predict the future. Only using credit cards in emergencies and paying the minimum fee by rotating the credit cards can allow a person to live for several years—depending on available credit—while maintaining a perfect credit history.

It's important to only apply for credit cards with no annual fee, and it's extremely important to have credit cards that offer balance transfer options. This will allow flexibility. Due to the declining real estate market, I was able to purchase a rental property for $35,000 with a credit card. I considered it a "good emergency." I was able to secure a balance transfer option from a major credit card, which allowed me to use up to 100 percent of my available credit with a two-year fixed interest rate of 0 percent, with only a 2 percent processing fee. This provided me the opportunity to collect rent for two years while I paid down the credit card balance. After two years, I will transfer the balance to another credit card with a 0 percent balance for another two years. After five years, I will have paid off my credit card with the rent I collected from the property. While the economy continues to decline, I will look for similar opportunities to strengthen my overall portfolio. The best thing about these opportunities is that I do not have to use my own funds because I have maintained a good credit history.

Credit reports are extremely important and should be part of a person's annual financial checkup. Due to the condition of the economy, identity theft has become more prevalent than ever. It is an individual's responsibility to protect his or her credit from predators. All three major credit bureaus—TransuUnion, Equifax, and Experian—offer free annual credit reports to all Americans with a credit history. These free credit reports can be obtained by calling (877) 322-8228. Obtaining and reviewing your credit on an annual basis can eliminate—or at least reduce—fraudulent transactions and unauthorized credit accounts being opened under a person's name. If you have been a victim of identity theft, you can add an extended fraud alert to your credit history file. If anyone tries to obtain credit under your name, you will be notified immediately. This is especially important because trying to prove that you have been a victim of identity theft can be extremely difficult and detrimental to your financial stability.

The only way to establish good credit is to pay your bills on time or in advance if you can afford it. Paying bills can be a very touchy and unpleasant subject. Everyone—rich or poor—has bills to pay, and if you are currently in a position where your bills are easily covered every month, you have already mastered the art of financial responsibility. When I got my first real job, I had to start paying my own bills, including rent to my mother. I look back fondly upon those good old days when I resided in my family's building. For several years, Millicent and I lived in a three-bedroom, 1,400-square-foot apartment, and the rent was only $300 per month. My portion was only $150. My mom taught me at a very young age that paying bills would always be a part of life.

My rent was due on the first of every month, and it was considered late after the third. However, instead of a late fee, I would be subjected to a lecture about financial responsibility, even in the presence of friends. The thought of having my mother burst in on me while I had company, demanding her rent or having me explain why the rent was late, was always a good reason to pay on time. After being late with the rent a few times, I learned a valuable lesson. I would rather learn discipline than be embarrassed in front of my friends. From that point on, I was never late with the rent again. My mother taught me that paying my bills on time was the best way to be spared from later embarrassment.

When I established various types of regularly recurring bills, I established a schedule. My payments were due on the fifteenth and the twenty fifth of each month. I put a system in place that I still follow today. I always planned ahead of schedule and made paying bills a priority. When I was a young adult, I would get paid at the end of every week. At the beginning of every month, I would calculate all my bills. Even if the bills were not due until the end of the month, I would make every effort to pay them before the fifteenth so I could use my last two paychecks in whatever manner I wanted.

My bills were more of a priority than spending money, hanging out with friends, or purchasing clothes and other items. From my last two paychecks, I would put away a little for the upcoming month's bills so that I always stayed ahead. If all my bills were paid by the fifteenth of the month, I would still have half my income left over to deposit into my savings account. As a young adult, I was already thinking about my future and how I could live well. I realized that the secret to success was to never limit or confine myself to a life that was defined by waiting for the next paycheck.

After paying all my bills with the first two paychecks, I put a little money away with the remaining two paychecks. A person who does not save for unexpected expenses will never save any money. It feels good to have all my bills paid and know that I still have a couple of checks coming in. I still follow this technique. The only differences are that I now get paid twice a month and my bills are now are ten times as much as they were—but so is the amount of pay. The discipline I had back then prepared me for the discipline I need today. I pay all my bills by the tenth of the month, my second paycheck is still free and clear to do with whatever I want, and I still save and invest.

While it is very important to always pay bills on time, if you are a little short of cash for the month, you should make every attempt to call your creditors, explain your circumstances, and request an extension or a payment plan. Requesting an extension or payment plan in most cases will not cause any adverse action on your credit history, and the extension or payment plan is usually granted because a creditor always prefers to collect payment rather than risking default.

It is important to always review bills for accuracy. The majority of the time, bills are correct, but I have still found computer errors on payment invoices that I have received. Although you may not have the time to review every item on your billing statements, you should certainly review the invoices with the highest charges. Take a glance at the amounts, terms of finance charges, and interest rates. I do not believe that creditors set out to take advantage of their consumers, but human and computer errors can occur. It is up to the consumer to catch any errors.

Creating a spreadsheet is helpful for paying monthly bills because it allows you to see where your money is being spent every month. It will also allow you to focus on certain items that you can try to lower. I have always used a yearly spreadsheet with a monthly breakdown of bills and expenses. My spreadsheet includes a snapshot of the entire year, and it calculates for the month while adjusting the total over the course of the year. At any given time, I can easily compare different months to see if my expenses are higher. This allows me time to research expenses and negotiate with the providers of my home, cellular phones, cable television, electric, and Internet. If any promotions are available, I can get a reduction in rate based upon my excellent payment history.

The spreadsheet is free, easy to create, and helpful because it lets me know when and where every dime is being spent. I can even see how much I spent five years ago for any given month. The spreadsheet tracks my monthly expenses, and it can track spending for entertainment on an ongoing basis. If you have a budget for spending and entertainment, a spreadsheet can help you manage your expenses. Creating a spreadsheet will help track your finances and make it easier to see where your money is being spent.

Rochelle Melanie

MONTHLY EXPENSE REPORT

Payee	Amount
Mortgage	$650
Assessments	$235
Automobile	$503
Home phone	$65.50
Mobile phone	$53
Electric	$120
Cable	$84.62
Gas	$75
Groceries	$139.42
Credit Card 1	$205
Credit Card 2	$69.84
Spending Cash and Entertainment	$250
Total	**$2,450.38**

CHAPTER 5
Banks, Finance Companies, and Loan Stores

WHEN BORROWING FUNDS, I PREFER banks to finance companies. Banks are financial institutions that provide many different services to their customers. These services include checking accounts for depositing of money and paying bills and savings accounts that allow a person to earn interest on deposits. Banks offer mortgages, investment opportunities, and auto, personal, and business loans.

When it comes to borrowing from a bank, I know up front what is being agreed to with respect to a prospective loan. Banks provide a more detailed description of finance charges and fees—with more favorable rates—than finance companies do. Finance companies mostly specialize in providing credit to customers who are looking to make purchases.

Finance companies do not offer checking or savings accounts. Finance companies usually take on higher-risk consumers who are looking for financing. Finance companies are more likely to approve credit at a higher rate for individuals who may have credit issues. Finance companies may charge lower interest rates, but they make the difference in finance charges and fees that consumers are often not aware of in advance.

Most people who are shopping for mortgages or unsecured loans will seek the lowest interest rate possible. However, most advertising makes lower numbers seem more appealing than they actually are in real terms. For instance, a price tag that reads $.99 looks more appealing than one that reads $1.00, but there is only a penny difference. An interest rate of 2.9 percent looks more appealing than 3.2 percent, but after looking closely at the closing costs and points available on both loans, the 3.2 percent interest rate may be cheaper than the 2.9 percent rate. It is important to understand all the closing fees in advance—*before* completing any transactions.

Banks disclose all this information prior to closing, but most finance companies do not. Bank closing fees are often standard and in a defined range, but fees from finance companies can vary greatly. Not all finance companies are out to take advantage of customers, but a lot of finance companies will take advantage of uneducated customers. The only benefit of choosing a finance company is when a person's credit history is undesirable, but the cost can be excessive. Many finance companies operate on the same level as used car salesmen who will sell pre-owned cars with a six- or seven-year loan with 22 percent interest to buyers with poor credit histories.

In loan stores, the exploitation of minorities is an ongoing social issue. Loan stores are located in the poorest communities. In my younger days, I often dreamed of owning my own bank, when neighborhood banks had a chance of survival. During the late 1980s, savings and loans were among the most popular financial institutions.

In those days, people could make money on deposits in checking, savings, and certificate of deposit accounts. It was common for people to receive interest rates of 10 percent on a certificate of deposit, which were savings accounts that had to be maintained for a certain period of time or a penalty would be assessed based upon the remaining time on the balance.

During that era, regular passbook savings accounts offered 6 percent to 7 percent interest rates, and checking accounts offered 3 percent to 5 percent interest rates. All of those bank accounts carried FDIC insurance up to $100,000 per account. When the savings and loan institutions started to fail, banks bought up the remaining savings and loan institutions as they became available. The days of the 10 percent interest rate started to vanish quickly. By the late 1990s, there were virtually no more savings and loan institutions.

In the next era, smaller banks merged, grew, and increased

revenues. During that time, the savings and loans institutions were devoured—and most small neighborhood banks had no choice but to merge with larger banks just to stay in existence. There was an increase in the community-banking sector during the first decade of the twenty-first century. For small banks, merging was not enough to keep them afloat because the entire banking industry was shifting.

Despite the size of a bank, it became evident that in order for a bank to survive it needed to be in the top ranking. When the banking industry became a little more stable—and the savings and loans intuitions were gone—the remaining small banks began to acquire other banks that appeared to be struggling. If a small bank were solvent, a larger bank in a stronger position would try to acquire it to strengthen its book size.

I worked for the last savings and loan institution that failed and was acquired by one of the largest banks in the United States. I have been through numerous mergers and acquisitions. It's interesting to go to work and have the federal government come through the front door and seize the entire company. The employees would be fired and rehired by one of the largest banking institutions in the United States. This certainly made for a very exciting workday. Being a part of the savings and loans institution era was a unique experience.

I am very familiar with the financial world, and I see loan stores popping up on every corner in low-income neighborhoods. In my opinion, loans stores are nothing but legalized loan sharking. The only difference between a loan shark and a loan store is that a loan store can rob people legally. There is nothing that can be done about this as long as someone has agreed to the outrageous loan terms by signing a contract.

The average low- to middle-income individual in a crisis will not be thinking logically and may have his or her judgment clouded when it comes to making financial decisions. The decision usually comes back to hurt the borrower. Loan stores prey on the less fortunate because they are the easiest targets—and often the most uninformed when it comes to financial matters. Several of my family members have borrowed money from loan stores and were faced with repayment amounts that were five times the original loan.

I reviewed the repayment contract of a friend who had borrowed $2,400 at a 32 percent interest rate. I have seen 28 percent and 36 percent interest rates on loans from loan stores. I reviewed another contract for a friend who had borrowed $2,000 and issued her car title as collateral. When she was unable to pay the money back, she lost her vehicle, which had been worth more than $9,000. Unfortunately, since those family members and friends did not come to me for advice before signing the contracts, there was nothing I could do to help them.

There are a lot of horror stories surrounding loan stores, and regrettably, these stores will continue to thrive in the poorest communities until minorities and low- and middle-income individuals start stabilizing their personal finances.

The loan stores do not care who is targeted—as long as a profit is being made.

I have thought seriously about opening up a loan store since establishing a small bank was no longer an option for me. In order to survive in the banking world, a privately owned institution would have to be among the top-ranking institutions. I thought that opening a loan store could be a quick, get-rich investment, but they totally disgust me because of how they exploit low- to middle-income individuals. Instead of adding to the problem, I decided to help fix the problem through education. My message to everyone is to avoid loan stores if at all possible. Do not let them take advantage of you; if given the opportunity, they certainly will.

CHAPTER 6

Coupons, Rebates, Reward Points, and Dollar Stores

MY SAVINGS STRATEGY INCLUDES USING coupons. I cannot tell you how many times I have heard wisecracks from my friends, peers, and family members when I pulled out a coupon. Since I was doing pretty well financially, they all thought that I would be the last person on earth to use a coupon. Wrong! I was the first person to always use a coupon. I used coupons for almost everything that can be imagined. I didn't hold up the grocery store line with a hundred coupons for every product in my shopping cart, but

I saved several hundred dollars every year by using valuable coupons for dining out, travel, clothing, household products, and so forth.

I absolutely love the Brownie Sundae Alamode at Dunkin Donuts. The smooth, rich, thick chocolate brownie with two scoops of ice cream, whipped cream, almonds, and a cherry costs $4.99 plus tax. One time, four of us were purchasing the same sundae, and the total came to $22 with tax. Everyone needed to pay $5.50, and each of us contributed our portion. When it was my turn to add my portion, instead of adding $5.50, I added $1.10 and a coupon that stated that my sundae would only cost 99 cents plus tax. We all had the same product. The coupon did not cost me anything. I saved $4.50, and the wisecracks stopped. This type of thing has happened many times with much higher savings. Every time I present my coupon, all the wisecracks stop. I use coupons at every opportunity because they cost me nothing but a minute of my time to clip them out of the newspaper.

My all-time favorite pastime is fine dining, and I dine out whenever I can. Dining out can be very expensive, but I can cut my costs in half with coupons. I have saved the most when it comes to fine dining because I'm always searching for special deals, coupons that offer the second meal free, or 50 percent off meals. This also comes in handy when it is my turn to pay.

Coupons can be found almost anywhere. You can get them online or clip them from magazines, newspapers, flyers, or entertainment books. During these stressful economic times, the savings are amazing. Coupons are great when it comes to saving money. The money that a person saves by using a coupon can reduce an overall bill. A coupon can be used to obtain additional products or services. If coupons are used when dining out, the savings can be used to cover taxes or a gratuity.

When I was starting out, I did not object to purchasing knockoff products to keep up with the latest styles. However, I learned very quickly that original items can be purchased "used" for a fraction of the full retail price. I prefer purchasing used items, and the money I save has been amazing. I deposit all the money I save by purchasing pre-owned items into my passbook savings account. I still have all the things I want, and I maintain a lavish lifestyle while living below my means. I have all the things I want without living from paycheck to paycheck. Throughout my life, I make smart purchases.

Who really wants to take the time to request a mail-in rebate? I do. Rebates may seem like a waste of time because they require locating rebate slips, cutting the proof of purchase from the box, filling out the rebate form, and mailing it to the company just to get a few dollars back, but they can be worth the effort. Most rebates require less than ten minutes. The task is tedious, but so are a lot of things that people do in life that are not mandatory. If all rebates were over ten dollars, perhaps more rebates would be mailed. The companies get to keep the money if the rebates are not mailed in. I always mail in my rebates. Some rebates can be as high as a hundred dollars. I view this as unanticipated income. It takes so long to receive the rebate that I usually have forgotten that it was coming.

It is it a nice surprise when I go through my mail and

have several refund checks that I had not been expecting. My favorite rebates make purchases almost free. When it is time to renew my virus protection on my laptop, I never renew online. I always go into the store. Electronics stores usually have the necessary software—with a sizable rebate. I have purchased software for $129 with a mail-in rebate of $99, making my final purchase price $30 plus tax.

Whenever I make a purchase and know I'm not going to return the product, the first thing I do is complete the rebate information and mail it. Over the course of the year, I have accumulated several products that are eligible for rebates, and I viewed them as discount or sale items. I have noticed that these little checks usually come in toward the end of the year, right around the holidays. When the checks start coming in, I think about how little effort it took to complete the rebate forms—and I feel grateful.

I also enjoy the reward points from my credit cards. A reward point basically allows a consumer to shop and travel for free—anywhere and at anytime. It is important to avoid credit cards with annual fees if possible. Annual fees on credit cards are a waste of money, especially when the credit card is not in use for long periods. Why pay for something that is not being used?

Several credits cards allow people to earn reward points that can be used toward future purchases. I use one credit card for all my everyday purchases so that I can accumulate as many rewards points as possible. Reward points allow me to get the items I want—but don't really need—for free. The points allow me to dine for free at nice restaurants. I also use the points for travel, and I pay nothing for them.

Some credit cards that allow holders to redeem points for travel may have annual fees, but if a person travels a lot, the annual fee can be worthwhile because it offers free airline travel. That is the only time I would make an exception of paying an annual fee. A person should always do research before selecting a credit card and always lean toward a credit card that offers reward points that can be redeemed for everything, including airline flights, merchandise, and dining.

The object is to save wherever you can. I always look for savings within my monthly bills and expenses. I call my creditors twice per month to see if there are any promotions or special discounts being offered that can help me cut back on the cost of my monthly expenses. I often find promotional discounts on my current services, which allow for a reduction for a certain period of time. If a person does not call, it is impossible to learn about promotions or discounts.

Filing appeals on property taxes is another way to save. Garage sales and online auctions are great ways to obtain money for items that have value. I'm also in favor of making trades for other items, repairs, or maintenance services. If an item has value, it is a good idea to try to get something for it. A person should not be wasteful and only buy things that are necessary. Hording, however, should never be engaged in when it comes to trying to save. A person should purge as often as possible in order to make room for things of value.

I had never been into a dollar store until recently. I was very surprised that I had not been in one of those stores sooner. I was expecting to see a lot of useless household items packed into cluttered isles with the smell of plastic everywhere, but I was amazed by the cleanliness and wide range of useful products in the store. As I browsed through the aisles, I found similar items to what I usually purchase—all for one dollar per item.

Dollar stores offer lots of savings when it comes to household items. I was particularly surprised when I purchased three greeting cards from a famous drug store that cost me $9.86. A friend insisted that I look at greeting cards in the dollar store across the street. I was surprised to find three nice greeting cards that cost a total of $1.58. I immediately returned the three greeting cards from the other store and got a refund. I purchase all my greeting cards—and many other items—at the dollar store.

If you have never gone to a dollar store, check one out. I'm sure you will have the same experience that I did. A lot of stores call themselves dollar stores, but everything in the store is not a dollar. If you look for a dollar store where everything in the store costs one dollar, you can go shopping and save.

CHAPTER 7
The Real Savings Begin Here

LEARNING ABOUT FINANCE MAY SOUND intimidating, but when it allows for the luxury of not worrying about how your bills are going to be paid, it should no longer seem to be so frightening. If a person earns a modest salary, this does not mean that he or she can not save money to accomplish his or her financial goal. This only means that he or she has to start out smaller and be wiser about his or her spending. My spending, savings and investing techniques are about making every penny count.

I started saving the coins I accumulated on a daily basis in my pockets. Every time I made a purchase, I never paid with the exact change. It's very easy to put change away because no one really wants to keep coins in a pocket or a purse. As soon as I got home, I discarded my pocket change. In that way, it was easy to accumulate several dollars worth of change in a short period of time.

When my piggy bank was full, I found a large plastic container that could not be opened without actually cutting off the top. I placed the two-foot container in my closet, knowing that when it was filled to capacity, it would be too heavy to move. I made it a practice to add change to my container every day. After a year, I noticed that my container was full. When

I decided to take my change to the bank, I had to separate the coins into four coin bags. I took the coins to the bank to have them counted since there was no charge for the service at the time. These days, most major grocery stores count coins.

After my coins were counted, I was surprised to learn that I had accumulated more than a thousand dollars. I was so impressed by the amount of change that I did not want to use the money on a vacation. I decided to open a passbook savings account. I bought a new container and started saving coins all over again.

I decided to deposit ten dollars from my weekly paycheck into my new passbook savings account—while continuing to save my pocket change. After my second year of saving coins and depositing ten dollars per week, I had $1,000 from the prior year's pocket change, $1,400 from the current year's pocket change, and $520 from my $10 weekly deposits. I had accumulated $3,120—plus interest from the passbook savings account—in two years. I had saved over $3,120 with virtually no effort at all. I knew it was the start of something great. I was well on my way to stabilizing my finances for the future.

I was so excited that I decided to start implementing other savings techniques. When I received annual pay increases and bonuses—no matter the amount—I added them to my passbook savings account. I decided to view all my pay increases and bonuses as if they did not exist. People cannot miss something that they have never had.

A person's standard of living should remain the same even after an increase or bonus. If I had lived for a year on a salary of

$15,000, I could continue to live on that salary; nothing should change because my salary had increased. Every year, I added my pay increase amount and any bonuses—after taxes—to my passbook savings. I continued to save my pocket change.

After five years of saving coins, adding the ten dollars per week to my checking account, and adding my pay increases and bonuses, I had accumulated more than $10,000. Seeing the extra zeros within my savings increased my drive to save more. The more zeros I saw behind my savings, the more zeros I wanted to see. In order to see more zeros, I knew that I had to become more aggressive with my savings.

Like any young adult, I wanted a car, nice clothes, and all the latest items that money could buy, but I kept my focus. If I could continue to save and pay now, I could definitely afford to play later. After filing my income taxes—before I had time to think of ways to spend my refund money—I immediately added the money to my passbooks savings account. I still save my pocket change, and I have increased my weekly deposits to twenty dollars. I add pay increases, bonuses, and income tax refunds to my savings. I'm on a roll now, and no one can stop me.

I live below my means and I did not go without any of life's bare necessities. Saving at least 20 percent of one's salary is clearly living below one's means, but it is necessary to accomplish a significant goal. The secret to saving is living below one's means while being able to manage financial responsibilities without stress.

I bought a car to get to and from work, I wore very nice

clothes that I often purchased on sale, and I had most of the toys I wanted, but I got them at a reasonable cost, which I will elaborate upon later.

As I got nearer to attaining my goals, I wanted to start reaping some of the benefits I had achieved at such an early age. I began to get more creative with my savings. When I was able to afford some of the nice things I wanted, I started to spend a little money, but I always tried to spend wisely. Whenever I made a purchase, I always selected quality over quantity. I only wanted the best for the best.

When I purchased my first automobile, I paid cash for a beautiful used, fully loaded Nissan sports car with very low mileage. I could have purchased a new car, but I based my decision on quality. As the years passed, I purchased another used vehicle with an extended warranty to cover anything that might go wrong. Why purchase a new car for thousands more if it depreciates in value and is considered used as soon as you drive off the lot?

Five years later, I purchased a new car because there were no used cars of the model that I wanted. It was a 1995 Chevy Camaro. Purchasing my dream car did not interrupt my savings at all. Before I purchased it, I made sure that I could afford it without changing my saving habits. After purchasing the vehicle, I discovered that I had a love for cars.

When I was a little girl, I watched my father build cars in his body shop. His skills were amazing. I'm convinced that my fascination with cars started then. My attraction to nice cars grew into an attraction to luxury cars; I always drive the best cars that money can buy. I keep all my automobiles for at least five years, and I get a full bumper-to-bumper warranty. Out-of-pocket repairs on luxury cars can be extremely expensive, and my plan is to save, not spend. It was an exciting time in my life. As a young adult, I owned a new car and a new Honda Elite scooter for casual driving around the neighborhood. As a young adult, I had options that were rare for someone of my age.

My dad retired from General Motors after thirty years of employment. In the nineties, all General Motors employees and their immediate family members were entitled to purchase new vehicles at invoice price. The additional employee discount percentage was another bargain for me. I saved a lot of money by using all the available options.

I continue to take advantage of all possible savings when it comes to high-end vehicles. It is possible to have a luxury vehicle if someone takes the time to research the available options and makes a smart purchase.

As a young adult, I also wore very nice clothes because my purchases were based on quality versus quantity. I often shopped at consignment and resale shops and found $500–800 suits for $100–200. After my purchases, I would take the suits to the cleaners to make sure they were properly cleaned. Once someone wore the clothes, they were considered used—why not purchase quality over quantity? When I had to purchase new items, I always shopped for bargains and sales. If the items I wanted were not on sale, I would periodically check to see if they had gone on sale or would make the purchase and look for the chance to get a credit or adjustment later. Those were a few more ways I was able to save.

CHAPTER 8
United States Savings Bonds

THERE WAS A TIME WHEN savings accounts paid relatively high interest rates, but those rates no longer exist. In order to live well without being wealthy, I had to revise my spending, savings, and investing techniques. The usual retail savings accounts would no longer be enough to make me financially stable.

I continued my monthly savings practices. After I paid all my bills and allowed for some spending cash, I began to purchase United States Savings Bonds.. Savings bonds are nonmarketable securities that can only be purchased or sold by authorized agents of the United States Treasury Department. A savings bond is a registered security that is owned by the individual or individuals who are listed on the face of the bond.

United States Series EE savings bonds are backed by "the full faith and credit" of the government, meaning that it is almost impossible for a person to lose the initial investment or accumulated interest due to the financial markets, unless the federal government totally fails. This was my next step to financial stability.

Income from savings bonds is not taxed at the local or state level, and the best feature is that while earning interest, there are no federal income taxes that need to be paid until United States savings bonds are redeemed, which used to take up to twelve years before the full maturity arrived. Another benefit of savings bonds is that if they are used for education, federal taxes do not have to be paid upon redemption.

Savings bonds can be a simple form of investing for anyone. A savings bond is purchased at half of its face value because the government is using the money to fund projects. Purchasing a savings bond at half of its face value allows the purchaser to earn that full face value amount while waiting for the bond to reach its maturity, which is the government's way of paying interest to the purchaser.

I started purchasing savings bonds when I was beginning to learn about various securities. At the time, my only savings had been my jar of coins and my passbook savings account, which was Federal Deposit Insurance Corporation (FDIC) insured. I started purchasing a savings bond every month in the amount of $25 with a face value of $50. The savings bonds had a maturity date of ten to twelve years.

The following year, I purchased fifty-dollar savings bonds

for a period of twelve months. As the years went by, I increased the face value amount of the savings bonds I bought to the next highest level. During the third year of purchasing savings bonds, I bought $37.50 bonds each month with the face value of $75. The next year, I purchased a savings bond every month for fifty dollars with the face value of a hundred dollars. I made these bond purchases every month, increasing the amount every year and stopping at the purchase amount of $2,500, with a face value of $5,000.

When I reached the $2,500 purchase cost, I started purchasing savings bonds every quarter instead of every month. After nine years, I had accumulated:

12 x $50 bonds = $600
12 x $75 bonds = $900
12 x $100 bonds = $1,200
12 x $200 bonds = $2,400
12 x $250 bonds = $3,000
12 x $500 bonds = $6,000
12 x $1,000 bonds = $12,000
4 x $5,000 bonds = $20,000
1 x $10,000 bond = $10,000

Because I increased my purchase amount over the years, I accumulated a total face value of $56,100 for the price of $28,050. I considered my bond purchases as safe money because I did not have to watch over them. It was nice to have the physical bonds in hand because it represented currency. United

States savings bonds no longer come in paper form. They are registered paperless book entries, but they still work in the same manner.

As times change, investment strategies have to change as well. After nine years of purchasing savings bonds, the maturity dates increased, which meant that I had to wait longer for the bonds to reach maturity. Also, the interest on the savings bonds started to decrease. I needed to become more aggressive. The savings bonds earned interest through their maturity, but the maturity dates increased from ten to twelve years to fifteen to eighteen years, which I do not consider a good investment. I still recommend saving bonds for beginning investors and children; however, other types of savings bonds are available for investing.

Savings bonds are considered to be credit-risk free because the government backs them. When a bond is considered credit-risk free, an investor does not have to worry about the issuer being able to pay interest or the principal amount that has been invested. When someone purchases a savings bond, the investment is protected by the nation's "full faith and credit."

Agency bonds are issued by institutions that were initially formed by the United States government to assist with homeownership and student loans, such as Fannie Mae, Freddie Mac, Ginnie Mae, and Sallie Mac. Municipal bonds, usually called *munis*, are sold to raise money for state and local government projects, such as toll roads, bridges, and police and fire departments. The best feature about munis is that investors usually do not have to pay federal income taxes upon them, and if the bonds are purchased in the same state where the individual resides, they are usually free from state and local income taxes.

Corporations issue corporate bonds for many reasons. These bonds have more credit risk than federal, state, or local government bonds. Corporate bonds will virtually always be taxable by both state and local government. Finally, junk bonds have a higher risk of default, but they also offer the potential of higher yields. Junk bonds typically have a lower credit rating which reflects the rating of the company that issues the bonds. Ratings are placed on bonds by popular companies such as: Moody's, Standard and Poor's, and Fitch.

I really enjoyed purchasing the United States savings bonds at half their face value and knowing that they were backed by the full faith of the United States government. The best feature is that a person can put the bonds away and not worry about them until maturity. This was part of my stable investment because there was no fluctuation within the face value, and they carry little or no risk.

CHAPTER 9
Mutual Funds

I CASHED IN MY SAVING BONDS, which had a face value of $56,100 and accumulated interest, and invested it in mutual funds. The mutual funds did not carry FDIC insurance or government backing, but they had the potential to grow at a faster rate of interest.

The feature I like best about mutual funds is that anyone can own them, and investors do not have to be financially knowledgeable to invest in these funds. Mutual funds have fund managers who help limit an investor's risk. Mutual funds can be risky, but they are a little more stable than investing in individual stocks.

Mutual funds are comprised of funds from thousands of

small investors. Fund managers buy stocks, bonds, and other securities with the collected funds. Participants contribute money to the funds to own a small portion of the entire investment. The majority of mutual funds allow a person to invest as little as $1,000. A manager will watch over the funds, which will be diversified among various stocks in one pool, and investors do not have to worry about constantly watching individual stocks. There are fees involved when someone purchases mutual funds, but these fees are typically over looked due to capital gains. Capital gains are increases of the original investment price. Capital gains can be short term which is appreciation in less than a year and long-term which is appreciation over a year. The appreciation on the investment is how capital gains taxes are assessed.

Some mutual funds can be started with almost any dollar amount, and most funds allow investors to make periodic deposits whenever they like. Deposits can be made weekly, monthly, or annually by automatic debit to take advantage of dollar cost averaging. Dollar cost averaging is an investment strategy that takes even monetary amounts regularly and periodically over an exact time period in an exact amount in a particular investment portfolio that allows shares to be purchased at a lower price as opposed to all the shares being purchased at a higher price. This strategy lowers the total price per share, giving the investor a lower overall cost for purchases over an extended period of time.

As mentioned, there are fees involved in purchasing mutual funds. There are thousands of mutual funds, and for beginning investors, most banks have investment advisors who can help select mutual funds to fit individual and family needs. Mutual funds have fund managers to manage the funds, but I do not advise beginners to invest without the help of an experienced financial investor.

When an investment is geared toward someone's financial future, it should not be considered for short-term gain. These types of investments are meant to be held for long periods of time in order to accrue marginal profits. Therefore, the proper amount of time should always be allotted, and for mutual funds an adequate time frame would be between six and ten years. The times when individuals could make large sums of money in a matter of days are long gone. This is why it is important to have the proper investments.

Investments are when a person put money into something with the expectation of growth—and the growth usually happens over a long period of time. When thinking about making investments, certain factors should be considered (goal, type of investment, comfort level, and amount). Start out at a comfortable level, and time should be allotted for research prior to making any investment. There are many ways to invest. There are also many types of investments, which include equities, market securities, options, hedge funds, commodities, exchange-traded funds, futures, gold, and real estate.

Most Americans lead very busy lives, but in order to live healthy, productive, and financially stable lives, we have to take the time to periodically review our finances. We have to make time to invest properly. In order to live well without being wealthy, those investments have to stay current because inflation can depreciate investments.

CHAPTER 10
The Stock Market

AFTER I CONVERTED ALL MY savings bonds to mutual funds, my capital gains were increasing at a more rapid pace. As a result, I decided to take advantage of the dollar cost averaging by setting up an automatic monthly deposit from my savings account to my mutual fund account.

Since I had the protection of a mutual fund money manager, I decided to focus on my next investment adventure. I opened up a brokerage account with my bank so that I could start trading on the major stock markets. I opened a brokerage account with only $1,000, and I started watching *Squawk Box* on Bloomberg TV every morning. I considered this financial source of information to be the most popular.

After I got dressed, I watched the pre–stock market opening television broadcasts for thirty minutes before I had to leave for work. I watched the ticker symbols at the bottom of the screen while listening to the news that surrounded some of the daily stock picks.

I learned very quickly that any important or breaking news—or even a presidential speech—could affect the stock market that day. Generally, if the news was positive, the market tended to rise (the bullish side). Negative news tended to make the market decline (the bearish side). The terms bullish or bearish are used to describe upward or downward movement within the stock market; this movement often reflects the entire market, but it can be seen separately in particular sectors of the market. There are all sorts of patterns to watch for in relation to investing in the stock market, and no pattern has a guarantee, but observing the relationship between breaking news and trends within the market worked for me.

As soon as I arrived at work, I studied my morning stock pick. Sure enough, my morning stock pick was usually right on target. I would study the high and low trends before I made my trades. I noticed that the highest time for the stock market was usually at the beginning of the trading day; the lowest time unusually happened around lunchtime in New York.

After taking some time to learn the stock market trends for the day, I would make my stock purchases. I usually focused on penny stocks, which are shares that are typically priced below five dollars per share, for relativity small companies with limited cash and capital. The stocks are usually somewhat high-risk investments with low trading volumes.

In my first trade, I purchased $1,000 of OPWV (Open Waive System) at the opening of the market. I watched my trade throughout the day, and when my stock doubled by midday, I sold it with a short-term capital gain of over $1,100. This was not bad for my first buy—and definitely not bad for only several hours of investing. This is how my day-trading experience began. Short-term capital gains occur when someone purchases a security and sells it in less than a year. Short-term capital gains taxes will be paid at someone's current income bracket level—as opposed to a flat tax rate for a long-term capital gain.

Day trading includes the purchase and sale of stocks or other investments—often within twenty-four hours—but I was trading between days and weeks. When I began trading on a regular basis, I entered the next phase of my financial life. Trading during my lunch hour at work quickly became my regular routine. I made sure I had enough time to watch *Squawk Box on* Bloomberg TV to see what was going on with the stock market before the opening bell.

On weekends, I would go to my favorite bookstore for several hours to catch up on financial news in the various magazines. I would grab several magazines, including my favorite, *Fortune.* I would have a handful of magazines, a cup of French vanilla coffee, and my laptop. I would spend hours researching and comparing my stock picks to the stock picks of Wall Street's greatest investors. The magazine section in Borders was the place to be on a weekend afternoon.

When Borders closed, I took it very hard because the store had been the best place to research and read whatever I wanted for free. I could never understand how the company stayed in business for as long as they did since it allowed people to do research and read books and magazines for hours without being obligated to make a purchase. Go figure! That was part of the bookstore's downfall, along with the emergence of e-books, which are becoming more popular every day.

Once I learned another way to invest, I would arrive to work earlier—and more eager than before. Trading allowed me to make money faster, without really putting in any hard work. I would get to work at six o'clock and log onto my computer as soon as possible to see what was going on with the premarket and to track my potential trades before the stock market opened. I would always make sure I had a couple of stock picks from the previous weekend. I would usually have two or three picks; how the picks were doing in the premarket would help determine how I would trade that day. Even with extensive research, trading can be extremely risky because no one can ever predict what is going to happen in the stock market on a daily basis.

Trading stocks became a large part of my investing, but I had been in the financial business for many years. ***I do not recommend or promote day trading for anyone.*** For individuals who are just starting to invest, I recommend mutual funds from a licensed broker. Mutual funds are used very diversely within a portfolio and are geared towards a long-term time horizon. I also urge everyone understand that any trading in the stock market can result in a loss of part or entire principal investment without the proper guidance.

My theory for the stock market is to never gamble with anything that you cannot afford to lose. With this theory in mind, and as much knowledge and advice a person can obtain, trading in the stock market the right way can produce a great benefit in the end. I do not want to discourage anyone from trading in the market. I just want people to be aware of the facts. Day trading is the most risky type of investing, and it requires a special skill and understanding. Even when a person possesses that skill, losses can still occur. I have certainly had my good and bad days as it relates to trading in the stock market.

Trading in the stock market certainly has its ups and downs. When the market is up, the rush is indescribable, but when the market is down, the rush can turn to panic. There were times when I was trading in heavy volume. I was trading every day while watching the market from open to close. I would start the day with my latest penny stock selection, and would only trade one stock at a time, which is extremely risky.

My usual trade of $1,000 per day increased to $10,000 per day. I quickly learned that the more money I traded, the higher my profit could be at the end of the day. I would start off my trade at $10,000, and depending upon how well my trade was doing, I would often let it carry on to the next day or the next week. The length of my trades averaged anywhere from a day to a week. I still considered it day trading because my gains were all in the short term (with a higher capital gains tax to pay at the end of the year).

When my trade amounts reached $20,000 per trade, I used the same cost basis over and over again. For example, if I placed a trade for $10,000 and made $20,000, my next trade would be for $20,000. My goal was to always increase my initial investment amount.

During my trading years, Krispy Kreme Doughnuts became the latest craving, and I became very interested in the product. The consumption of these doughnuts by American consumers was amazing. After learning that this company was about to go public, I did a lot of research. I decided to go see the only Krispy Kreme factory, which was on the South Side of Chicago.

I was totally amazed when I saw the factory. Lines of cars extended for blocks. The storefront was made of glass so people could see employees making the doughnuts. Customers were buying the doughnuts fresh from the fryers by the dozen. I could not believe what I was seeing. This craving was totally out of control.

I waited in line and observed the cars increasing behind me. There appeared to be no end to the line. When it was my turn, I purchased a dozen doughnuts. Surprisingly, I was not that impressed. I placed a whole doughnut in my mouth, and it collapsed within a second. The doughnuts were hollow and covered with sugar. I was able to eat a whole doughnut in less than two bites. I could not understand the craving for this clump of sugar, but it did not matter that I did not like the product. It was important that everyone else did; the sales of these doughnuts were amazing.

After I concluded my research, I wanted to be a part of what could be one of the biggest initial public offerings (IPO) of all time. Companies initiate IPOs in an effort to raise capital by selling shares to the public. When Krispy Kreme went public, I could not participate in the IPO because of my position at the bank. I had to wait for the stock to hit the open stock market before I could make a purchase.

In preparation, I stopped my regular trading in order to have all my cash free and clear to purchase as much Krispy Kreme stock as possible. When Krispy Kreme stock hit the open market, I purchased 1,439 shares at various prices. I bought and sold the stock for six months with the same initial investment amount. When Krispy Kreme reached an all-time high, the company decided to do a two-for-one split, reducing the price of the stock and making more shares available to the public at a lower price while increasing the equity of the company. Over the course of six months, my Krispy Kreme investment made me approximately $18,000. While I was enjoying my short-term gains from Krispy Kreme, the stock started to slide.

The popular trend of eliminating carbohydrates from people's diets to lose weight had an effect on the Krispy Kreme stock. Americans started to embrace the Atkins Diet, which promotes rapid weight loss by eliminating carbohydrates. It was the start of the decline of Krispy Kreme's stock price. Being the investor that I was, it was time for me to let go of Krispy Kreme and move on to other stocks, such as (WAVX)-Wave System Corp, (ASTM)-Aastrom Biosciences, Inc., (VTSS)- Vietesse Semiconductor Corp, (MSFT)- Microsoft Corporation, (WU)- The Western Union Company, and (ILMN)-lllumina, Inc.

which would continue to net me thousands of dollars on a weekly basis.

After many more successful years of trading, I was doubling my annual salary from the bank. I continued to trade and was always on the lookout for the next great IPO, but I did not find one again until many years later. Google stock hit the open market at approximately $85 per share. Google was considered the biggest IPO in history, and it has reached a high of over $920 per share. I thought that Facebook would be the next big IPO, but thus far, it has been a little disappointing. However, I have still not ruled it out.

Several years after the World Trade Center attack on September 11, 2001, several large companies collapsed due to insider trading allegations—and the financial markets became extremely risky. Tight restrictions were placed on financial institution employees and their immediate families. These tight restrictions made it difficult for individuals like me to day trade. Employers began implementing restrictions that forced traders and their immediate families to hold securities for a certain period of time before they could be sold.

I could purchase the same type of securities, but I had to hold the securities for a minimum of thirty days before I could sell them. Before the restrictions, I could make a purchase or sale without a holding period. It became a requirement to obtain approval from management to trade. This type of trading was not conducive to my style of conducting transactions. This type of trading limited me in many ways, as if I had lost my second income stream. It was time for me to move on to another type of investing.

Since all my savings and investments had derived from my pocket change, I felt as if I was back at the beginning—but with much larger pockets this time around. I decided to try it their way. After a year, my profits were much smaller—and the chances of making $10,000 in a couple of months were gone. In order to help things along with the declining market, I developed my own way of dollar cost averaging while investing in the stock market. Dollar cost averaging is a process in which a person who purchases a stock is taking the risk of loss of principal, but if someone knows what he or she is doing, rewarding profits can also be made. I'm like the average investor; I do not invest in the stock market with the idea that I'm going to lose my principal.

It is important to have the proper experience or guidance because the stock market is not FDIC insured and loss of principal can occur.

During a bullish or bearish market, I wait until prices have stabilized, which allows my investments time to work for me. After the market has calmed down and I have an unrealized loss for a certain period of time, I start to do my own dollar cost averaging. I look at the price and the number of shares I purchased, and I wait until I see the price at its lowest value. I repurchase the same amount of shares over and over again until I bring the original cost of the shares down to its lowest point. Then I sell the entire lot at its highest price with a profit, instead of selling at a loss.

For example, I bought 100 shares of ABC stock for $50 per share (100 shares x $50 = $5,000). If my shares declined in value to $30, then I purchased another 100 shares at $30 per share (100 x $30 = $3,000). I own 200 shares, divided by $8,000, which equals $40 a share instead of $50. If I continue this method every time the stock decreases in value, I can eventually sell at a profit instead of a loss. This method takes time—and usually will not generate a lot of profit—but it helps prevent me from selling at a loss.

The difference between most inexperienced or new investors and me is that I'm very patient. Many inexperienced or new investors get caught up in thinking about the old days of making a fast dollar, but those times are long over. I think the biggest mistake by investors who start to see their investments decrease in value is panicking and selling the stocks. Inexperienced or new investors think they are losing money, but they only encounter a paper loss until the stock is actually sold. Inexperienced or new investors think that a downturn in the stock price is the right time to pull out of the market, and the first thing they do is sell and realize a loss. When the market is declining in value, it is the perfect time to buy because stocks are considered to be on sale. Inexperienced or new investors need to understand that the market will fluctuate.

My favorite part of investing—and my largest gains—came from trading in the stock market. I had to go through all the other steps of saving and investing before I started trading in the stock market because I did not have the experience of investing in the stock market. Investing in the stock market is riskiest form of investing, but it can be the most lucrative. *I want to make it very clear that I do not recommend day trading to anyone.* I recommend investing in the stock market with the advice of an experienced licensed investor while having the understanding that any investments in the stock market should be based on long-term strategies.

Any trading a person does in the stock market can result in a loss of part or the entire principal investment.

CHAPTER 11
Real Estate

I CONVERTED ALL MY POCKET CHANGE that I saved over the years to cash. I opened a passbook savings account and started depositing ten dollars per paycheck into my savings account, increasing the amounts as the years passed. I purchased savings bonds every month after all my bills were paid and increased the amounts of these purchases each year to the next denomination. When the maturity dates increased on savings bonds, I cashed in all my accumulated saving bonds and transferred all my money from my passbook savings account into a mutual fund that is being actively managed. I moved to the next level of investing, which was trading in the stock market. After making profits for so many years trading, and with all the new restrictions that were placed on trading, it became time to find another investment avenue.

I have always taken time to look at my finances and see how I can increase my wealth in any way. I moved away from home, where I was paying a small amount of rent to my mother every month, at the age of twenty-five. I have never paid rent to anyone else for a property I did not own. I bought a foreclosed condominium in 1995 for a very good price in Oak Park, Illinois, which is one of the best western suburbs in the state. I made all the necessary repairs to my property for a little over five thousand dollars.

At the age of twenty-five, I had a beautiful spacious condo in a wonderful area with a mortgage payment of less than $500 per month because I had been saving and was able to put down a sizable deposit. I lived in that condo for ten years, and when the stock market started to decline, I decided to look into purchasing investment properties.

My primary residence was purchased at a very reasonable price with a built-in cushion of equity. Over the years, the property increased in value. By 2008, the property had increased to an appraised value of three times its original cost. I decided to apply for a home equity line of credit. With the equity in my home and my excellent credit history, I was able to secure a fairly high line of credit. As I mentioned earlier, credit plays a very critical role in your financial wealth because it can be used in many ways.

Real estate was never my passion because it involved more work than I wanted to commit to in my busy life. Real estate was my mom's passion. After obtaining my line of credit, I did extensive research and purchased my first investment property. I also consolidated a few bills to increase my cash flow.

Purchasing my first income property was the start of a new investment adventure. As the economy started to suffer, the real estate market became saturated with inexpensive properties for sale. Over the years, I have made other real estate investment purchases—and continued to increase my net worth. I look at buying investment properties as though my primary residence had given birth to a couple of baby properties. I used the equity from my primary residence, and there were no additional out-of-pocket costs for me. The rental income is paying back the funds I borrowed, which were secured by the equity to make the purchase.

Real estate can be purchased through any licensed real estate agent or broker. Foreclosed property listings are available to the public and can be found by doing some research on the Internet. The real estate market is currently in an extremely ghastly state; as a result, I was able to purchase a beautiful property for $35,000 with a credit card that offered me a 0 percent financing for almost two years (with an incredibly small service fee). Since I used a credit card, I did not have to obtain a mortgage from a bank. I did not have to go through a lengthy closing process, and my overall closing costs were minimal.

The significance of maintaining a good credit history cannot be overstated. A good credit rating can make it possible for a person to take advantage of very good real estate investments.

CHAPTER 12
401(k), Deferring Income

A 401(K) IS A QUALIFIED RETIREMENT plan that is established by an employer into which eligible employees can make salary deferral contributions on a pretax and after-tax basis. Pretax contributions are taken from a pay check before (gross) any other taxes are taken. After-tax contributions are taken from a paycheck after (net) all other taxes have been taken. Employers offering these types of plans often make matching or nonelective contributions to them on behalf of eligible employees.

Most 401(k) retirement plans have company matches of deposits, the ability to make pretax contributions, choices of investment selections, the ability to contribute up to 15 percent of an employee's pay before or after taxes, and company bonuses. A 401(k) retirement plan is geared toward retirement; therefore, all investments should be made with a long-term goal in mind.

A 401(k) retirement savings plan does not allow withdrawals until the age of 59½ without penalty. There are certain circumstances that may permit a withdrawal without penalties, including financial hardship, education tuition, a new home purchase, or a loan from the plan in which the borrowed amount is paid back (usually through an automatic debit from payroll).

The 401(k) retirement plan is a unique investing plan that consists of mutual funds, and it is not free. The mutual funds have fund managers. The fund managers are proactively watching the overall mutual fund investments, and the investments in the portfolio are growing aggressively (depending on the selections that are made).

There are fees associated with purchasing mutual funds. A person should always pay close attention to the fund manager's fees. The mutual fund fees are not the most visible because the fund manager's fees are embedded within the actual funds. The average person who is investing in the 401(k) retirement plan or mutual funds usually does not pay attention to the fees because the appreciation within the mutual fund portfolio is usually the focus.

Investors who look at the bottom line and see growth do not care about what it cost—unless they find out that the bottom line could have been much higher. Mutual fund fees are important, but I would not spend a lot of time worrying about them. I would certainly try to keep the overall fees lower than 1.5 percent; this will make a major difference in the growth of your portfolio over time. I personally believe that the 401(k) retirement plan is one of the best retirement saving plans because of its many benefits.

When I started working for my company, there was a three-year waiting period before a new hire could join the company's 401(k) retirement plan. Three years seemed like a long time, and it also seemed like I was missing out on a big opportunity to invest in my future. As soon as the three-year waiting period was over, I enrolled in the 401(k) retirement plan.

As a young adult, one of my major concerns was bringing home as much net income as possible. Tax-deferred contributions did not mean anything to me. I was only concerned with my net income. A tax-deferred contribution is when monies are taken from a paycheck before any taxes are deducted. It also means that a person can defer any tax payments until retirement as long (as there are no taxable withdrawals made from the plan before the age of 59½). Some companies allow employees to retire at an early age, and exceptions are made regarding withdrawals from the plan.

After the first year of contributing to my 401(k) plan, I saw the matching contribution and the capital gains and decided to increase my contribution amount. I continued to increase my contribution every year until I finally reached the maximum of 15 percent pretaxed.

Most companies allow employees to make after-tax contributions. After-tax contributions are made after all the taxes have been taken from a person's paycheck—and the contribution is made with net income. The major difference between the pretax contribution and the after-tax contribution is the bottom line deduction from a person's paycheck. The pretax contribution does not appear as significant as the after-tax contribution in a person's net take-home pay.

I slowly made after-tax contribution over time. My pretax contributions, after-tax contributions, company matches, bonuses, and incentives to join helped increase the value of my portfolio in many ways. Since most young adults don't know that retirement will be here before they know it, saving for retirement is the last thought on their minds. The 401(k) retirement plans have many benefits; the pretax and tax deferral features are the most popular because they allow individuals to save for retirement with the least amount of impact on their take-home pay.

While saving for retirement, another important thing to remember is that a person should have at least six months of reserve funds in the event of job loss, which is calculated by totaling monthly expenses and saving six times that amount for a rainy day. In the event of a job loss, this will be a cushion while seeking employment. Unfortunately, during unstable financial times, people may have to increase this to a one-year reserve fund. The unemployment rate is very high, and it is taking double—and often triple—the amount of time to find employment. The reserve fund may take time to build because of regular savings, but people will benefit from having a backup plan in the event of losing a job.

I have invested in the 401(k) retirement plan since I was a young adult, knowing that I will retire eventually. I stopped being concerned about my bottom line take-home pay. I invested with pretax and after-tax dollars while reinvesting my capital gains. Needless to say, my 401(k) retirement investment plan has grown significantly. The 401(k) retirement investment plan has added another layer to my saving and investing. A

401(k) retirement plan is another investment that can help secure a person's financial wealth.

At the beginning of a person's career, it is important to participate in all the savings plans that a company offers—even if the person can only afford 1 percent.

CHAPTER 13

Investing with Life Insurance

EVERYONE SHOULD HAVE LIFE INSURANCE—OR at least the bare minimum of burial insurance. Life insurance can be used in many ways and too often low- to middle-income individuals only think of it as an insurance policy that is paid after the death of the insured for burial services.

Wealthy Americans often use life insurance as an investment strategy to build financial wealth. This type of investing is very savvy and is designed in a manner that is difficult to understand. Therefore, most low- to middle-income individuals tend to avoid this type of investing.

Life insurance can be an effective way of creating wealth and passing down a significant amount of wealth to one's heirs. Many legacies have been created through life insurance policies.

The types of life insurance can vary in many ways. A few of the most popular options are term life, whole life, universal life, permanent life, group life, accidental death, limited pay, endowments, and annuities.

Term life insurance is the most basic form of insurance, and it is strictly purchased for the death of the beneficiary and has no accumulated cash value. Term life insurance is often the most inexpensive policy a person can purchase. Many employers use this type of insurance at a low premium because this type of insurance usually terminates after employment has ended.

Whole life insurance offers a lifetime benefit. This type of insurance starts off at a reasonable rate, but it can become expensive when the policyholder gets older. Employers also offer this type of life insurance at a higher premium rate. Unlike term life insurance, whole life insurance can follow a person after termination of employment, but the premium usually doubles. Whole life insurance does have a cash value and guaranteed death benefits. The policyholder of whole life insurance is entitled to the cash value reserves. The policyholder can access the cash reserves through loans.

Universal life insurance is a policy that combines permanent insurance coverage and a flexible premium. The growth potential of the cash value reserves is often greater. I really like that universal life insurance premiums and death benefits are flexible, unlike whole life insurance policies where premiums and death benefits are fixed. The insurance benefits can be increased or decreased, but this will require underwriting approval. Having the ability to adjust premiums can be beneficial during difficult times.

Group insurance is exactly as it states; it covers an entire group of people. Companies of all kinds generally use this type of insurance. An insured person who leaves the group can purchase individual insurance for continued coverage. The group life insurance premium is sometimes paid in part by the employer and the employee.

Permanent life insurance is a permanent policy that cannot be canceled by the insurance company. This type of insurance remains in effect until the policy matures (unless the policyholder fails to pay the required premiums). This policy has a cash value, and the policyholder can make withdrawals and loans against the cash value reserves.

Limited-pay insurance is a permanent insurance that is based on how insurance premiums are paid over a period of time. The premium payments are usually paid between ten and twenty years.

Accidental death insurance is usually referred to as (AD&D) accidental death and dismemberment. This type of insurance is strictly used in the event of an accident or dismemberment of the insured. Accidental death and dismemberment insurance can be inexpensive, depending on the person's occupation. An investment banker, accountant, or a school teacher will pay less than a skyscraper window washer, firefighter, or military service member because of the nature of their jobs.

Most insurance policies can be purchased, and AD&D coverage can be added to the policy for an small premium rate.

The best benefit of AD&D insurance is the double indemnity. Double indemnity is paid if the insured died as a result of an accident. If the insured had a life insurance policy with death benefits of $50,000 and died accidentally, the beneficiary will receive $100,000. The $50,000 is paid for the general death, and the additional $50,000 is paid for the accidental death.

My favorite insurance policies to invest in are endowments and annuities. Endowment insurance policies are designed to pay a lump sum at maturity or at the death of the insured. The maturity date of an endowment policy usually ranges from ten to twenty years. Endowments have a specific amount of accumulated cash value that is equal to the death benefits, depending on age. Endowments are used as investment vehicles, and the premium payments on endowments are usually much higher than those on all the other insurance policies referenced above.

Annuities are another form of insurance in which tax-deferred premiums are paid by the annuitant. Insurance companies insure annuities, and an annuitant can receive payments immediately or later in life. Annuities offer a lot of flexibility, and withdrawals from an annuity can be taxed.

Endowments and annuities are commonly used as investment vehicles. Using insurance polices as part of an investing strategy to build financial wealth requires a very special skill set that often involves a licensed insurance representative. This does not mean that using insurance policies should be avoided; it simply means that the average person will need help with this type of investing.

Investing with life insurance is how the wealthy increase and maintain their financial wealth. As I mentioned earlier in this chapter, the average person only views insurance polices as family protection against death of a loved one, and they rarely think of using insurance polices as investment tools. In order to build financial wealth, this thinking has to change.

THE END RESULT

PEOPLE MAY WONDER WHAT DIFFERENCE it makes where financial wealth originates. Knowing the origin of wealth can only strengthen a person's knowledge about the best way to obtain financial wealth.

Most Americans think that financial wealth comes from working long, vigorous hours or even working two jobs. Working a regular nine-to-five job without a proper saving and investing plan is the least effective way to become financially stable, but it is a good starting point for anyone. The average American will not inherit a trust fund or a large sum of money, will not receive the proceeds of a lawsuit, or be the beneficiary of a substantial life insurance policy. Average Americans work regular nine-to-five jobs, and those jobs are usually their only sources of income. The only way a regular job could possibly equate to financial wealth is through the proper saving and investing of income.

Few Americans are able to achieve financial wealth through their jobs, but they usually do not have ordinary jobs. They usually have specialized careers that allow them to earn large salaries. Unfortunately, the average low- to middle-income American struggles with finances. Understanding how wealth is accumulated and making the necessary adjustments will increase the chances of being successful and achieving goals. Knowing the origins of wealth can be essential to a person who is trying to build wealth because it provides directions.

Leaving a legacy of financial knowledge is just as important as leaving financial wealth. Leaving a legacy without financial wealth teaches descendants how to create new wealth. A person may not inherit financial wealth, but knowing how to earn and manage financial wealth is important for success.

The most important thing to remember about legacies is that they do not have to be financial. Many people have inherited financial wealth and lost everything in a short period of time because they did not have the skills to maintain it. What is the point of inheriting financial wealth if it is going to be squandered?

The biggest mistake that is made by parents or loved ones is passing down financial wealth to an individual who is incapable of understanding how to preserve it. If a parent decides to pass down financial wealth to an uneducated beneficiary, a trust fund should be considered. A trust fund can protect the child from squandering the inheritance until the child is ready to handle the responsibility of managing financial wealth.

Teaching children how to manage money will allow them to maintain inherited financial wealth as adults. Knowledge costs nothing and can be passed down from generation to generation. What difference does it make if people mismanage money that could have supported them for the rest of their lives? In that case, the purpose of the inheritance has been defeated. Anyone can learn how to obtain wealth or manage inherited wealth.

The primary focus for the average American is working to support a family. The majority of Americans rely on their jobs to provide for their families, and this is where a good work ethic can play an important role in life. Maintaining a good work ethic allows a person to stay employed and to be marketable. Being employed and marketable allows a person to earn income to pay bills, save, and invest whatever is left over.

A lot of Americans take funds straight out of their paychecks for saving and investing. The average nine-to-five job may not make a person wealthy, but the income stream that it provides will allow a person the opportunity to save and invest. In order for a person to start saving and investing, there must be income. One of the best ways to produce an income stream is through employment. In order to maintain an income stream, a person has to have a good work ethic, which is achieved by going to work on time, performing at one's best, and going above and beyond the regular work duties in the workplace.

Organization is a must; without organization, there is no structure. Personal and professional organization allows a person to set goals and standards. A person needs to have a strategy in place. If people organize their plans ahead of time and work at achieving those goals in order of importance, their success rates are usually high.

People should create strict guidelines for staying professionally and personally organized. Having good credit is a part of being organized. Maintaining a good credit score enables a person to establish credit, which can be beneficial in building wealth. In order to establish good credit, people must always pay their bills on time.

Good credit can be more beneficial than cash because it can extend much further than cash when it comes to certain purchases. The average person has always viewed cash as the best means for purchasing, and this is true—except when it comes to purchasing high-ticket items, such as real estate and automobiles.

Good credit makes a huge difference when it comes to borrowing from banks, finance companies, or loan stores. Most banks offer more favorable rates and fees to individuals with good credit. Banks may also offer reasonable rates and fees to individuals with less desirable credit. Finance companies are willing to work with individuals with less desirable credit. Loan stores are a legal way to take advantage of people with no justice to follow. They prey on the unfortunate in their times of need. Loan stores have the highest possible rates when it comes to short-term lending. Loan stores are meant to be a short-term cash-flow fix, but the interest rates on the loans seem to escalate the problem for borrowers even more.

Coupons, rebates, reward points, and dollar stores are other ways to save. Taking a few minutes to cut out coupons, fill out rebate forms, redeem reward points, or shop at a dollar store can save a person a lot of money over the years. They may not seem like they save a lot of money, but over the course of a year, the savings can add up significantly.

Reward points are my favorite. I enjoy fine dining, and reward points allow me to enjoy my favorite restaurants more often. I try to use my credit card for every single purchase so I can accumulate as many reward points as possible. I look for promotions that offer double points or extra ways to earn additional points. Every few months, I redeem my points for restaurant cards or cash back, which I use for dining. I pay my credit card bill in full every month to avoid any interest charges. I make sure that my credit cards have no annual fees—and that I'm receiving the best possible rate. I enjoy the fact that I can use my reward points for dining and entertainment and can save my money for investing.

It may seem hard to believe that I accomplished all this by saving pocket change. I always knew that my pocket change would equate to something significant over time. Saving my pocket change, converting it into a passbook savings account, and depositing ten dollars per week into my savings started it all. Paying all of my bills monthly and purchasing savings bonds with the leftover funds—while increasing the savings bond amounts every year—was the third layer of my savings and investing plan.

Understanding and keeping up with inflation allowed me to recognize when I needed to make a change in my investing strategy. Investing in my company's 401(k) retirement plan allowed me to take my savings and investing to another level when the savings bond industry was no longer an attractive investment due to increased maturity dates. Adding mutual funds introduced me to the stock market. The mutual funds were a pool of stocks that balanced each other. If certain stocks within the mutual fund were underperforming, the other stocks could balance out any losses.

When I entered into the big leagues, I purchased individual stocks from the various stock exchange markets. The stock market is the riskiest form of investing, but it was the most profitable form of investing for me. I'm a firm believer of not investing what you cannot afford to lose.

I studied, planned, and monitored every stock I purchased. I made the most profits in the shortest amount of time. I had some principal losses, but day-trading losses should be expected at some point. Purchasing individual stocks is the riskiest type of investing that I have ever done. When the stock market was no longer profitable in the way that I was accustomed to it being, I gravitated to a more stable investment, which was real estate. I purchased low-cost properties when they were available. The real estate market became my stable investment, and then I added insurance to my portfolio. Adding a little insurance to my portfolio took some strategic planning, but it was worth it.

I still reside in my very first real estate property, which I purchased fifteen years ago. While saving for my first property, I took the time to decide where and how I wanted to live. I strategized and perfected a plan that would work for me. I did not purchase until I had saved up a nice down payment, and I moved only after I found the perfect place. I purchased very economically and restored the property to my liking. I have the perfect location—and a space that works for me.

My friends ask why I do not upgrade, because they feel I surely can afford to. I always say, "Yes. I can afford to upgrade, but why should I if I am comfortable?"

I'm a strong believer that people should never conform to the spending habits of others just because they can. A person should do whatever feels comfortable—despite his or her net worth. I have always done what was comfortable for me, and I never tried to compete with others.

When the economy spiraled into a recession, it did not affect me in any way because I have always done what was comfortable. A couple of my friends have serious financial burdens. One friend who had a net worth of a couple million dollars is almost homeless. Other friends have huge financial burdens because they conformed to society's norms for the upper class. They lived above their means just to stay up with the current trends.

I set a plan in motion, and I stayed on course. Eventually, I will move into the house of my dreams—but not because I want to stay current with society. I refuse to be in a position of poverty if I can help it, and this is accomplished by living below one's means until financial goals are met.

The most important thing to remember is that a person does not have to be wealthy or a millionaire to live well. A person has to be smart about spending, saving, and investing. My pocket change grew into a savings account, then it grew into savings bonds, then into mutual funds, then into stocks, then into real estate, and then into insurance polices. I invested in my company's 401(k) retirement plan. I lived below my means by using coupons when I shopped, filled out rebates whenever they were offered, and took advantage of reward points for my fine dining experiences, which saved me money that I used for investing. I paid all my bills on time and maintained a perfect credit score to get low rates on loans and purchase real estate. In order to do all of this, I stayed employed, healthy, and organized. The best part about this accomplishment is that it started with pocket change.

There are many ways to invest, and I have just scratched the surface of the types of investing that have allowed me to become financially stable. Saving smart requires techniques that begin with knowing how to save on any income. A person should never be discouraged about starting off small because the goal is to end up big—this is why every penny counts.

I'm just like the average American, but I learned how to save and invest with a small amount. Low- to middle-income individuals have to save and invest differently from the wealthy because they do not have the same resources. I started off with an annual salary of $7,600, and I was able to achieve my goals by saving, investing, and watching what I spent. I did it—and everyone else can too!

Open Book Editions
A Berrett-Koehler Partner

Open Book Editions is a joint venture between Berrett-Koehler Publishers and Author Solutions, the market leader in self-publishing. There are many more aspiring authors who share Berrett-Koehler's mission than we can sustainably publish. To serve these authors, Open Book Editions offers a comprehensive self-publishing opportunity.

A Shared Mission

Open Book Editions welcomes authors who share the Berrett-Koehler mission—Creating a World That Works for All. We believe that to truly create a better world, action is needed at all levels—individual, organizational, and societal. At the individual level, our publications help people align their lives with their values and with their aspirations for a better world. At the organizational level, we promote progressive leadership and management practices, socially responsible approaches to business, and humane and effective organizations. At the societal level, we publish content that advances social and economic justice, shared prosperity, sustainability, and new solutions to national and global issues.

Open Book Editions represents a new way to further the BK mission and expand our community. We look forward to helping more authors challenge conventional thinking, introduce new ideas, and foster positive change.

For more information, see the Open Book Editions website: http://www.iuniverse.com/Packages/OpenBookEditions.aspx

Join the BK Community! See exclusive author videos, join discussion groups, find out about upcoming events, read author blogs, and much more! http://bkcommunity.com/